A Vegan Taste of Thailand

Also by Linda Majzlik

Vegan Baking

Vegan Barbecues and Buffets

Vegan Dinner Parties

A Vegan Taste of The Caribbean

A Vegan Taste of France

A Vegan Taste of Greece

A Vegan Taste of India

A Vegan Taste of Italy

A Vegan Taste of Mexico

A Vegan Taste of The Middle East

A Vegan Taste of North Africa

A Vegan Taste of Eastern Europe

A Vegan Taste of Thailand

Linda Majzlik

Jon Carpenter

Our books may be ordered from bookshops or (post free) from
Jon Carpenter Publishing, Alder House, Market Street, Charlbury,
England OX7 3PH

Credit card orders may be phoned or faxed to 01689 870437
or 01608 811969

First published in 2004 by
Jon Carpenter Publishing
Alder House, Market Street, Charlbury, Oxfordshire OX7 3PH
☎ 01608 811969

Reprinted 2009

ISBN 978 1 897766 92 7

Printed in England by CPI Antony Rowe, Chippenham

CONTENTS

Rice

Noodles

Curry pastes and curries

Vegetables

Salads

Accompaniments

Desserts

Fruit cocktails

INTRODUCTION

Thailand, which until 1939 was known as Siam, covers an area of nearly 200,000 square miles and lies at the heart of mainland Southeast Asia. Because of its shape, Thais affectionately describe their country as the 'elephant's head', with the trunk forming a thin peninsula that borders Malaysia in the south. The country is geographically diverse and the forested mountains in the north give way to gently sloping hills and fertile plains in the central and southern parts, where an abundance of crops including several types of rice and a huge variety of vegetables and tropical fruits thrive in the hot climate.

Thailand's economy is based on agriculture and it is estimated that up to 75 per cent of the work force earn their living from the land. Typically much of the food is produced on small-scale farms or smallholdings and this kind of farming forms the basis of the traditional Thai community. Although much produce is exported, most notably rice and tropical fruits, a lot of what is grown finds its way daily to the myriad colourful and lively outdoor markets, where Thai cooks can choose from the freshest locally-grown ingredients to create their distinctively flavoured dishes.

While Thailand has remained fiercely independent, its cuisine has over the centuries been influenced by various other traditions, most notably by China, where a large proportion of the population originated, and also by the neighbouring countries Burma, Laos, Cambodia and Malaysia. Western influences have also played a part in shaping the cuisine and the use of chillies may date back to the 16th century, when they were first introduced by traders and missionaries from Portugal. The main religion in Thailand is Buddhism, but there are many Muslims in the southern provinces. Their ancestors are believed to have come from the Indian subcontinent and the foods enjoyed in the south tend to be hotter and spicier than those served in the north, with roti, an Indian-style flat bread, popular as an accompaniment for curries. All these influences have resulted in a colourful and exotic style of cooking that is widely praised for its great balance of flavours and textures and its imaginative presentation. Even the simple act of garnishing a dish has become an art form in Thailand. Fruits and vegetables are carefully and intricately carved and used as edible decorations.

As in all countries in Southeast Asia, Thai meals have no separate courses and all food is served at the same time, for diners to help themselves to. Rice is the centrepiece, and all the other dishes are arranged around it. Thai people consider it a great misfortune to eat alone, as the sharing of food is looked upon as a source of joy. They also prefer to eat a little of lots of different dishes rather than a lot of a single dish and the more people who share a meal the greater the variety of foods that can be enjoyed. Thai cooks aim to achieve a harmonious blend of textures, flavours and colours and a typical meal might consist of the rice dish, a soup, a couple of vegetable dishes, a curry, a salad and at least one sauce. Food is eaten with a fork and spoon and black tea or coffee may be served to round off the meal. Sweet dishes tend to be eaten as snacks during the day, but Thais sometimes finish their meal with fresh fruit.

Veganism may be virtually unheard of in Thailand, but with many of the typical dishes already suitable for animal-free diets and certain others easily adaptable, there is no reason for vegans to miss out on this exciting cuisine. Many of the ingredients used will already be familiar to vegan cooks and other Thai-style ingredients are becoming increasingly easy to obtain. Thai cuisine offers vegans great scope, especially if they are in a hurry, as many of the dishes are very quick and easy to prepare.

THE VEGAN THAI STORECUPBOARD

As the popularity of Thai cuisine continues to increase in the west, it is becoming much easier to buy Thai-inspired ingredients. Although shopping for us may not be as exciting as choosing the ingredients from the lively markets and floating stalls that are such an important part of Thai culture, it does mean we can experiment at home and create some authentic-tasting vegan Thai dishes.

Bamboo shoots Used in stir-fries and salads, young bamboo shoots are readily available in tins, either whole or sliced. They simply need to be drained and rinsed before use. Any bamboo shoots left over can be frozen.

Brown sugar Palm sugar, obtained from the sap of the coconut palm, is used to balance the flavours in all kinds of savoury Thai dishes. Hard blocks of palm sugar that need to be broken into useable pieces can be bought from Oriental grocery stores and some delicatessen. If it is difficult to find, soft brown sugar makes a good substitute.

Cashew nuts A good source of protein and minerals, cashew nuts are roasted to enhance their flavour and used whole, halved, chopped or ground as an ingredient or for garnishing. Bowls of cashews are often served as part of the main meal and they are also eaten as a snack.

Chillies As well as forming the basis of Thai curry pastes, numerous Thai recipes use either fresh or dried chillies. The type that is most popular in Thailand is known as bird's-eye chillies, which are tiny but extremely hot. If these are unavailable other small chillies can be substituted. Fresh chillies keep well in the fridge for up to 10 days, while dried chillies can be stored for several months in an airtight jar.

Coconut An essential ingredient in Thai cuisine, coconut adds a creamy richness and distinctive flavour to sweet and savoury dishes.

Creamed This is pure fresh coconut flesh, shaped into a block and vacuum-packed. Once opened the block needs to be kept in the fridge and used within a couple of weeks. Alternatively, for longer storage, grate the whole block and put it in an airtight container in the freezer.

Flaked Flakes of dried coconut are lightly toasted to make them more flavourful and then used to garnish sweet and savoury dishes.

Milk A rich thick liquid made from pressed coconut flesh, available tinned or in cartons. Coconut milk can also be made by dissolving 4oz/100g grated creamed coconut in 20 fl.oz/600ml hot water or by blending 6oz/175g desiccated coconut with 20 fl.oz/600ml hot water and straining it through a fine sieve or muslin bag, pressing out as much liquid as possible. As well as thick and thin tinned varieties, reduced fat versions are becoming increasingly available. Many packets of coconut powder for making into milk contain animal products, so check the ingredients carefully. Any unused coconut milk can be frozen.

Cornflour A very fine starchy white flour milled from maize, sometimes called cornstarch. It is used for thickening sauces.

Curry paste It can be quite difficult to find ready-made vegan Thai curry pastes, as many varieties contain fish sauce or shrimp powder. Shop-bought pastes can also be much hotter than home-made versions.

Dried mushrooms Valued for their rich intense flavour, dried mushrooms need to be reconstituted in warm water. The varieties favoured in Thai cuisine include black fungus and shiitake, although other less expensive types can be used instead.

Galangal This looks like root ginger and is a member of the same family, but has a slightly pink tinge and a more subtle flavour. Fresh galangal is used in much the same way as root ginger and can be frozen. Dried galangal is often more easily available than fresh and two dried slices can be used instead of a 1 inch/2.5cm piece of fresh galangal. Ground galangal is also available, but this should be avoided as the taste is not comparable.

Ginger, root An essential Thai flavouring, root ginger is used to add warmth and a spicy, fragrant taste to numerous savoury dishes. It is a vital ingredient in many Thai curries and stir-fries and is occasionally used to flavour sweet dishes and drinks. Grated raw ginger is sometimes used as a garnish or simply mixed with soy sauce as a condiment. To store root ginger, cut into portions, wrap individually in foil or cling film and freeze.

Ginger, stem Stem ginger preserved in sugar syrup is available in jars. This sweetened version makes a popular addition to fresh fruit salads and other dessert dishes.

Groundnut oil Also known as peanut oil, this inexpensive, bland cooking oil is preferred for frying as it can be heated to high temperatures without burning.

Ground roasted rice This is made at home (see page 102) and used as an ingredient in sweet and savoury dishes.

Herbs Not many herbs are used in Thai cuisine, but those that are, either as an essential ingredient or as a garnish, are always used fresh.

Basil As well as sweet basil, other varieties such as hairy and holy basil are regularly used. The leaves are shredded and used fresh, or fried until crispy and used as a garnish.

Coriander A uniquely flavoured herb that is used extensively as an ingredient and as a garnish. Thai cooks not only use the leaves, but in certain recipes also the root.

Mint Whole leaves are often added to flavour salads made from mixed green leaves and whole and chopped leaves are used for garnishing.

Kaffir lime leaves A type of lime grown in Thailand and commonly used in Thai cuisine. The leaves of the plant impart a fresh lemon-lime flavour to all kinds of dishes. Fresh leaves can be bought in Oriental grocery stores and they freeze well. Dried leaves are more readily available and have a long shelf life if stored in an airtight container.

Lemon grass Indispensable in many Thai recipes, fresh lemon grass stalks have a fibrous texture and they need to be trimmed and finely chopped or blended before being used. The stalks impart a fresh, aromatic lemony flavour and are a vital ingredient in Thai curry pastes. Jars of ready-made purée are readily available and if fresh stalks are hard to find bottled whole stalks can be chopped and substituted. Dried lemon grass should be avoided as the taste is quite different.

Mung beans These tiny, green-skinned creamy-flavoured beans are a good source of protein and are the most popular beans for sprouting. Rather than being used whole, cooked mung beans are more likely mashed to a purée and then used in both savoury and sweet dishes.

Noodles An ever-increasing range of noodles is appearing on shop shelves and luckily for vegans, many of these do not contain eggs. With most noodles only needing to be soaked in boiling water for about 4 minutes before use, they can form the basis for some very quick and easy to prepare meals.

Peanuts A crucial ingredient in the Thai kitchen, peanuts are an excellent source of protein and are always roasted to enhance their flavour. Used chopped or ground to add texture and flavour to a whole range of dishes, bowls of peanuts are also served alongside the main course as a condiment and widely eaten as a snack food.

Rice The staple food of Thailand, rice is always the centrepiece of the main meal. Many types of rice are grown and enjoyed, but the most highly prized is Thai jasmine rice, a fragrant, long grained variety which has become increasing popular in the west and is now easily obtainable.

Rice flour pancakes Used for wrapping around savoury fillings, these rigid pancakes need to be soaked in hot water for about 20 seconds to make them pliable. Once filled the pancakes may be served cold, steamed or fried.

Rice vinegar White, black and red vinegars are distilled from rice. The white variety is often most readily available and is used in recipes here. It imparts a mild aromatic flavour to all kinds of savoury dishes.

Rice wine This richly flavoured seasoning is occasionally used in dressings and other savoury dishes. It can be bought in some supermarkets, but a medium sherry makes a good substitute.

Sesame oil A rich, thick, golden oil made from roasted sesame seeds which has a unique aroma and an intense nutty flavour. It is widely used for seasoning and gives an authentic Thai flavour to all kinds of savoury dishes.

Sesame seeds These tiny protein-packed seeds are roasted to enhance their flavour and used as an ingredient or to garnish dishes.

Spices Certain spices are essential for making Thai-style curries and these should be bought whole and ground at home in a mortar with a pestle.

Black pepper Whole peppercorns are freshly ground to season savoury dishes.

Cardamom This pine-fragranced spice is available in three forms, as pods, seeds or ground. The pods vary in colour, but it is generally agreed that the green variety is most flavourful and aromatic. The seeds are used in some rice dishes and curries.

Cinnamon Used as sticks or ground, cinnamon has a warm, sweet flavour and is used in curries and dessert dishes.

Cloves Ground cloves are considered an essential flavouring in mussaman curry paste.

Coriander seeds With a mild, sweet, orangey flavour, coriander seeds are an essential ingredient in Thai curry pastes.

Cumin seeds Another necessary ingredient in Thai curry pastes, cumin has a strong earthy flavour. Ground cumin is occasionally used in spicy snack food recipes.

Turmeric This bright yellow spice is the powdered rhizome of a plant belonging to the ginger family. It adds colour and a pleasant earthy flavour to curries and rice dishes.

Soy sauce Made from fermented soya beans, with light and dark versions available. Dark varieties have a richer, more intense flavour. Both types are used as flavouring and also served in little bowls as condiments. For the best flavour choose brands that are made from whole soya beans rather than from processed soya.

Soya milk Unsweetened soya milk has been used in the few recipes requiring it.

Straw mushrooms These tiny dome-shaped mushrooms have a distinct woodland flavour and are readily available in tins. They simply need to be drained and rinsed before being used whole or sliced.

Tamarind purée The acidic-tasting fruit of a large tropical tree, tamarind is used to add sourness to savoury dishes and drinks. Jars of ready-made purée are available and sticky blocks of crushed tamarind pods can be found in specialist shops. These need to be soaked in hot water to produce a purée.

Textured vegetable protein A nutritious and versatile soya product which readily absorbs the flavours of other ingredients. The natural, unflavoured variety is used in recipes here.

Tofu A complete vegetable protein food made from soya beans. Tofu has been a valued food in the Far East for centuries and it is enjoyed in various forms in hot and cold dishes. Although ready-marinated pieces can be bought, it is often more economical to buy blocks of plain tofu to marinate at home (see page 35).

Vegetable stock Invaluable when making soup and numerous other dishes, vegetable stock is easy to make and adds a more authentic flavour than stock cubes. It can be made in bulk and frozen in measured quantities. Prepare and chop a selection of vegetables such as carrots, celery, beansprouts, shallots or onion, leek, peppers, radishes and dried or fresh mushrooms. Put them in a large pan with some chopped chilli and garlic, a few sprigs of fresh coriander and some black peppercorns and cover with water. Bring to the boil, cover and simmer for 30 minutes. Strain the liquid off through a fine sieve.

Water chestnuts These crunchy, nutty-flavoured tubers are sometimes available fresh in Oriental grocery stores, but they are more easily found tinned and these just need to be drained and rinsed before use.

SOUPS

Most Thai soups are very quick and easy to prepare and are made from an exciting mix of fragrant spicy flavourings and fresh nutritious ingredients. Rather than being served as starters, soups are an integral and essential component of the meal and are eaten along with all the other dishes. Heartier soups are commonly served as snacks throughout the day or as breakfast or supper dishes.

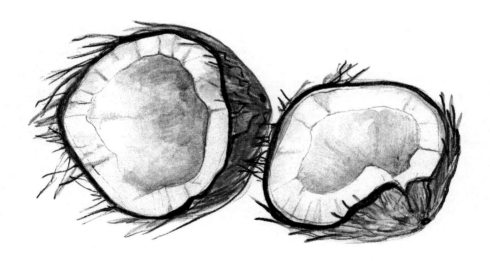

Courgette, cashew and bamboo shoot soup (serves 4)

12oz/350g courgette

4oz/100g tinned bamboo shoots, drained and cut into diagonal
   slices

4 shallots, peeled and finely chopped

2 garlic cloves, crushed

1 green chilli, deseeded and finely chopped

1 lemon grass stalk, finely chopped

2oz/50g roasted cashew nuts, ground

6 kaffir lime leaves

1 tablespoon lime juice

1 tablespoon brown sugar

1 dessertspoon groundnut oil

24 fl.oz/725ml vegetable stock

black pepper

extra roasted cashew nuts, chopped

shredded fresh basil leaves

Cut the courgettes lengthways into thin slices and cut each slice into 1 inch/2.5cm diagonal strips. Fry the shallots, garlic, chilli and lemon grass stalk in the oil for 3 minutes. Add the courgettes, lime leaves and juice, brown sugar and vegetable stock, bring to the boil, cover and simmer for 5 minutes. Then add the bamboo shoots and ground cashews and season with black pepper. Stir well and continue simmering for a few minutes until the courgette is tender. Ladle the soup into serving bowls and garnish with chopped cashew nuts and shredded basil leaves.

Coconut, tofu and noodle soup
(serves 4)

8oz/225g plain tofu, finely diced

4 shallots, peeled and chopped

2 garlic cloves, chopped

1 lemon grass stalk, chopped

1 tablespoon soy sauce

1 tablespoon groundnut oil

1 dessertspoon lime juice

1 dessertspoon brown sugar

2 dried bird's-eye chillies

black pepper

4oz/100g wheat noodles, broken into short lengths

2oz/50g creamed coconut, grated

24 fl.oz/725ml boiling water

2 kaffir lime leaves

toasted flaked coconut

Put the shallots, garlic, lemon grass, soy sauce, groundnut oil, lime juice, sugar and chillies in a small blender and blend smooth. Pour into a saucepan and add the tofu. Mix well, then cover and chill for at least 2 hours to marinate. Dissolve the creamed coconut in the water and add to the pan. Season with black pepper, stir well, add the lime leaves and bring to the boil. Put in the noodles and simmer gently for 5 minutes. Serve the soup in bowls, garnished with toasted flaked coconut.

Rice and pepper soup (serves 4)

4oz/100g long grain rice

4oz/100g red pepper, finely sliced

4oz/100g yellow pepper, finely sliced

4 shallots, peeled and finely chopped

2 garlic cloves, crushed

1 tablespoon groundnut oil

30 fl.oz/900ml vegetable stock

1 rounded dessertspoon tamarind purée

black pepper

crispy fried garlic (see page 102)

1 inch/2.5cm piece of root ginger, grated

spring onion rings

Cook the rice, rinse under cold running water and drain. Fry the red and yellow peppers, shallots and garlic in the oil for 3 minutes. Add the stock and tamarind purée, season with black pepper and bring to the boil. Cover and simmer for 3 minutes, then add the rice and simmer for 2 minutes more. Ladle the soup into serving bowls and garnish with crispy fried garlic, grated root ginger and spring onion rings.

Peanut and green vegetable soup (serves 4)

1lb/450g prepared mixed green vegetables (e.g. courgette, green pepper, green beans, broccoli), chopped into even-sized pieces

2 shallots, peeled and finely chopped

1 garlic clove, crushed

1 inch/2.5cm piece of galangal, finely chopped

2oz/50g roasted peanuts, ground

1 rounded tablespoon green curry paste (see page 68)

1 tablespoon groundnut oil

1 tablespoon lime juice

22 fl.oz/650ml vegetable stock

4 kaffir lime leaves

black pepper

chopped fresh coriander

Heat the oil and fry the shallots, garlic and galangal for 3 minutes. Add the curry paste and stir around for 1 minute. Now add the vegetables, lime juice, stock and lime leaves and season with black pepper. Stir well and bring to the boil, then cover and simmer, stirring occasionally, for 5 minutes. Stir in the ground peanuts and continue simmering for a few minutes until the vegetables are tender. Serve each bowl of soup garnished with fresh coriander.

Beansprout and lettuce soup (serves 4)

6oz/175g beansprouts

6oz/175g Chinese leaves, shredded

4 shallots, peeled and finely chopped

2 garlic cloves, crushed

1 inch/2.5cm piece of root ginger, finely chopped

1 small red chilli, deseeded and finely chopped

1 tablespoon groundnut oil

1 dessertspoon lemon grass purée

26 fl.oz/775ml vegetable stock

4 kaffir lime leaves

black pepper

crispy fried garlic and shallots (see page 102)

Fry the shallots, garlic, ginger and chilli in the oil until soft. Add the Chinese leaves and stir around for 1 minute, then put in the beansprouts, lemon grass, stock and lime leaves and season with black pepper. Stir well and bring to the boil. Cover and simmer for 3 minutes, then ladle the soup into bowls and garnish with crispy fried garlic and shallots.

Mixed vegetable and rice noodle soup (serves 4)

4oz/100g leek, trimmed

4oz/100g carrot, scraped

4oz/100g courgette

4oz/100g red pepper, thinly sliced

2oz/50g flat rice noodles, broken into short lengths

1 garlic clove, crushed

20 fl.oz/600ml vegetable stock

1 tablespoon groundnut oil

1 dessertspoon soy sauce

1 rounded teaspoon lemon grass purée

½ teaspoon crushed dried chillies

4 kaffir lime leaves

black pepper

finely grated lime zest

chopped fresh coriander

Cut the leek, carrot and courgette into 2 inch/5cm long ribbon strips and stir-fry them with the red pepper and garlic in the oil for 5 minutes. Add the vegetable stock, soy sauce, lemon grass purée, chillies and lime leaves and season with black pepper. Stir well, bring to the boil, then add the noodles and simmer for 5 minutes. Garnish the bowls of soup with lime zest and chopped coriander.

Pumpkin and coconut soup (serves 4)

1lb/450g pumpkin flesh, diced

4 shallots, peeled and chopped

1 lemon grass stalk, chopped

1 inch/2.5cm piece of root ginger, chopped

2 garlic cloves, chopped

1 small red chilli, deseeded and chopped

4oz/100g red pepper, thinly sliced

1 tablespoon groundnut oil

1oz/25g creamed coconut, grated

4 fl.oz/125ml hot water

15 fl.oz/450ml vegetable stock

1½oz/40g roasted peanuts, finely chopped

2 kaffir lime leaves

black pepper

fresh basil leaves

Blend the shallots with the lemon grass, ginger, garlic and chilli until smooth, then fry in the oil for 5 minutes. Add the pumpkin, red pepper, vegetable stock and lime leaves and stir well. Bring to the boil and simmer for about 10 minutes until the pumpkin is just tender. Meanwhile, dissolve the coconut in the hot water. Add this to the soup with two-thirds of the peanuts, season with black pepper and simmer for another minute. Serve in bowls, garnished with the remaining peanuts and some basil leaves.

Carrot and ginger soup (serves 4)

1lb/450g carrots, scraped and cut into 1 inch/2.5cm matchsticks

4 shallots, peeled and finely chopped

1 inch/2.5cm piece of root ginger, finely chopped

1 dessertspoon groundnut oil

1 dessertspoon soy sauce

black pepper

24 fl.oz/725ml vegetable stock

finely chopped roasted peanuts

grated root ginger

Fry the shallots and chopped ginger in the oil for 2 minutes. Add the carrots, soy sauce and vegetable stock and season with black pepper, stir well and bring to the boil. Cover and simmer for about 5 minutes, until the carrot is cooked. Garnish each bowl of soup with chopped peanuts and grated root ginger.

Curried wheat noodle and vegetable soup (serves 4)

4oz/100g broccoli, chopped

4oz/100g red pepper, sliced

2oz/50g tinned sliced bamboo shoots, drained

2oz/50g wheat noodles, broken into short lengths

4 shallots, peeled and finely chopped

2 garlic cloves, crushed

1 inch/2.5cm piece of galangal, finely chopped

½oz/15g creamed coconut

1 rounded tablespoon red curry paste (see page 68)

½ teaspoon turmeric

1 dessertspoon lime juice

1 dessertspoon soy sauce

30 fl.oz/900ml vegetable stock

1 tablespoon groundnut oil

black pepper

chopped roasted peanuts

green chilli rings

Heat the oil and fry the shallots, garlic, galangal and red pepper for 3 minutes. Add the curry paste and turmeric and stir around for 1 minute, then put in the broccoli, stock, lime juice and soy sauce and season with black pepper. Combine well and bring to the boil, cover and simmer for 5 minutes. Stir in the noodles, bamboo shoots and coconut and simmer for a further 5 minutes, stirring occasionally. Ladle the soup into bowls and garnish with chopped peanuts and chilli rings.

Mixed mushroom soup (serves 4)

6oz/175g mixed fresh mushrooms, wiped and sliced

½oz/15g dried mushrooms

4 shallots, peeled and finely chopped

1 lemon grass stalk, finely chopped

½ red chilli, deseeded and finely chopped

2 garlic cloves, crushed

10 fl.oz/300ml boiling water

16 fl.oz/475ml vegetable stock

1 dessertspoon groundnut oil

1 dessertspoon soy sauce

1 dessertspoon lime juice

1 dessertspoon brown sugar

4 kaffir lime leaves

black pepper

finely chopped fresh coriander

Soak the dried mushrooms in the boiling water for an hour. Fry the shallots, lemon grass, chilli and garlic in the oil until soft, add the fresh mushrooms and fry until the juices begin to run. Then add the soaked dried mushrooms and soaking water, vegetable stock, soy sauce, lime juice, sugar and lime leaves and season with black pepper. Stir well and bring to the boil. Cover and simmer for 5 minutes, and serve the soup in bowls garnished with chopped coriander.

Spicy courgette and corn soup (serves 4)

8oz/225g courgette, cut into 1 inch/2.5cm matchsticks

6oz/175g baby corn, cut into ½ inch/1cm slices

4 shallots, peeled and finely chopped

2 garlic cloves, crushed

1 inch/2.5cm piece of galangal, finely chopped

1 rounded tablespoon yellow curry paste (see page 69)

1 dessertspoon groundnut oil

4 kaffir lime leaves

16 fl.oz/475ml vegetable stock

black pepper

yellow chilli rings

finely chopped fresh coriander

Fry the shallots, garlic and galangal in the oil until softened. Add the curry paste and stir around for 1 minute. Stir in the courgette, baby corn, lime leaves and vegetable stock and season with black pepper. Raise the heat, cover and simmer gently for 10 minutes, stirring occasionally, until tender. Garnish each bowl of soup with yellow chilli rings and chopped coriander.

SNACKS

Snack foods are an integral part of Thai cuisine and culture and a vast array can be bought in towns and cities all over Thailand from street vendors, who sell their wares from permanent or mobile stalls. Some of these snacks are ready-prepared and simply displayed in huge baskets, carried around by vendors on foot or on bicycles, while other dishes are quickly made to order in elaborate stalls that are more like mobile kitchens. Snack foods can even be purchased from boats which are paddled up and down the waterways and many Thais are said to travel long distances to seek out their favourite food sellers.

All this activity has become a great tourist attraction and at certain times of the year stallholders are kept busy day and night to satisfy demand. Along with the following examples, other foods that are popular as snacks include noodle, rice and dessert dishes.

Aubergine, rice and cashew nut balls (makes 18)

12oz/350g aubergine, finely chopped

4oz/100g long grain rice

4oz/100g roasted cashew nuts, ground

1 onion, peeled and finely chopped

2 garlic cloves, crushed

1 lemon grass stalk, finely chopped

2 tablespoons groundnut oil

1 tablespoon red curry paste (see page 68)

2 tablespoons finely chopped fresh coriander

black pepper

cornflour

extra groundnut oil

Cook the rice until tender, drain and allow to cool. Fry the aubergine, onion, garlic and lemon grass in the 2 tablespoonfuls of oil for 10 minutes, stirring frequently, then add the curry paste and stir around for 1 minute more. Remove from the heat and mix in the cooked rice, ground cashew nuts and chopped coriander. Season with black pepper and combine thoroughly. Take rounded tablespoonfuls of the mixture and shape into balls. Roll each one in cornflour and pat off excess. Put the balls on a plate, cover and chill for a couple of hours, then fry them in hot oil for a few minutes until golden. Drain on kitchen paper and serve hot with a dipping sauce.

Savoury coconut pancakes (makes 8)

4oz/100g plain flour

10 fl.oz/300ml thin coconut milk

4 shallots, peeled and grated

2 garlic cloves, crushed

2 dried bird's-eye chillies, crushed

black pepper

groundnut oil

Mix the flour, shallots, garlic and chilli with the coconut milk, season with black pepper and whisk until well combined. Oil a 6 inch/15cm non-stick frying pan with groundnut oil and heat until hot. Put 2 tablespoonfuls of the mixture in the pan and swirl around until it spreads evenly over the base. Fry for a few minutes, then carefully turn over and cook the other side until golden brown. Repeat with the remaining mixture to make 8 pancakes. Serve with a salad topping and a savoury sauce.

Tofu and tamarind dip (serves 4)

4oz/100g firm tofu, finely chopped

2oz/50g tomato, skinned and chopped

2 shallots, peeled and finely chopped

2 garlic cloves, crushed

½ red chilli, deseeded and finely chopped

1 dessertspoon groundnut oil

1 rounded dessertspoon tamarind purée

2 fl.oz/50ml water

1 rounded teaspoon brown sugar

black pepper

Fry the shallots, garlic and chilli in the oil for 2 minutes. Add the tofu and tomato, fry for a further 3 minutes, then remove from the heat. Dissolve the tamarind purée in the water and add to the pan together with the sugar. Season with black pepper, pour into a blender and blend smooth. Spoon into a serving dish and allow to cool. Serve with a selection of thin sticks of celery, cucumber and carrot, tomato wedges, spring onions, and mushroom and radish slices.

Sweet potato and peanut cakes (makes 10)

1lb/450g sweet potato, peeled and diced

2oz/50g roasted peanuts, ground

2 shallots, peeled and grated

1 garlic clove, crushed

1 inch/2.5cm piece of root ginger, grated

1 dried bird's-eye chilli, crushed

black pepper

groundnut oil

Steam the potato and mash smooth. Add the ground peanuts, shallots, garlic, ginger and chilli and season with black pepper. Mix very well, then take heaped dessertspoonfuls and roll into balls in the palm of the hand. Flatten the balls slightly and chill them for 2 hours. Shallow fry the cakes in hot groundnut oil for a few minutes on each side until browned. Drain on kitchen paper and serve hot with a sauce.

Sesame and soy fried nuts (serves 4)

2oz/50g shelled blanched peanuts, halved

2oz/50g cashew nuts, halved

1 teaspoon sesame oil

1 teaspoon light soy sauce

1 dried bird's-eye chilli, crushed

Put the nuts, sesame oil and chilli in a small pan and mix until the nuts are coated in oil. Gently fry the nuts, stirring continuously, until they begin to brown. Add the soy sauce and stir well, then turn out into a serving bowl and allow to cool.

Sweet and sour stuffed spinach leaves (makes 16)

16 young spinach leaves

filling

2 limes

2oz/50g roasted peanuts, chopped

1oz/25g creamed coconut, grated

2 shallots, peeled and finely chopped

2 inch/5cm piece of root ginger, grated

2 garlic cloves, crushed

1 green chilli, finely chopped

2 tablespoons finely chopped fresh coriander

1 dessertspoon rice vinegar

1 dessertspoon brown sugar

black pepper

Peel the limes and remove all the pith, membranes and pips. Chop the segments finely, put them in a mixing bowl with the remaining filling ingredients and mix thoroughly. Wash and dry the spinach leaves and place a rounded dessertspoonful of filling on each one. Roll the leaves up to enclose the filling and secure with a cocktail stick. Arrange the stuffed leaves on a plate and serve with a dipping sauce.

Fried mung balls (makes 22)

4oz/100g mung beans

4 shallots, peeled and grated

2 garlic cloves, crushed

2oz/50g ground roasted rice (see page 102)

2 dried bird's-eye chillies, crushed

1 rounded teaspoon ground cumin

1 tablespoon lime juice

1 dessertspoon light soy sauce

black pepper

groundnut oil

Cook the mung beans, drain in a sieve and press out excess liquid with the back of a spoon. Put the beans in a bowl and mash smooth, then add the shallots, garlic, ground rice, chilli, cumin, lime juice and soy sauce. Season with black pepper and combine thoroughly. Take heaped teaspoonfuls of the mixture and roll into balls, put these on a plate, cover and chill them for 2 hours. Shallow fry the balls in hot groundnut oil until golden brown, then drain on kitchen paper and serve hot with a sauce.

Corn and potato cakes (makes 18)

8oz/225g sweetcorn kernels

1lb/450g potatoes, peeled and cut into chunks

2 spring onions, trimmed and finely chopped

2 garlic cloves, crushed

4 rounded tablespoons finely chopped fresh coriander

1 dessertspoon light soy sauce

black pepper

cornflour

groundnut oil

Steam the potatoes and mash them in a mixing bowl. Blanch the sweetcorn for 2 minutes, drain and roughly mash. Add to the potato together with the spring onions, garlic, coriander and soy sauce, season with black pepper and mix thoroughly until everything binds together. Take rounded dessertspoonfuls of the mixture and roll into balls in the palm of the hand. Roll each ball in cornflour, then flatten them slightly. Shallow fry the cakes in hot groundnut oil for a few minutes on each side until golden. Drain on kitchen paper and serve hot with a sauce.

Marinated tofu (serves 4)

8oz/225g plain firm tofu, diced

1 inch/2.5cm piece of root ginger, grated

2 garlic cloves, crushed

2 dessertspoons light soy sauce

1 dessertspoon sesame oil

1 dessertspoon lime juice

Mix the ginger with the garlic, soy sauce, sesame oil and lime juice. Add the diced tofu and combine well. Cover and refrigerate for about 4 hours, stirring occasionally. Transfer to a serving bowl and serve as a snack, or add to noodle dishes.

Peanut and rice fritters (makes 20)

4oz/100g roasted peanuts, ground

4oz/100g ground roasted rice (see page 102)

4 shallots, peeled and finely chopped

2 garlic cloves, crushed

1 teaspoon dried chillies, crushed

1oz/25g creamed coconut

6 fl.oz/175ml hot water

black pepper

groundnut oil

Mix the peanuts with the rice, shallots, garlic and chilli in a bowl. Dissolve the creamed coconut in the water and add, season with black pepper and combine very well. Cover and leave for 1 hour. Take rounded dessertspoonfuls of the mixture and fry in hot groundnut oil until golden. Drain on kitchen paper and serve hot with a dressing or a dipping sauce.

Fried spring rolls (makes 8)

8 rice flour pancakes

6oz/175g plain firm tofu, finely chopped

4 spring onions, trimmed and finely chopped

2 garlic cloves, crushed

½ inch/1cm piece of root ginger, finely chopped

1 tablespoon roasted sesame seeds

1 dessertspoon sesame oil

1 dessertspoon dark soy sauce

1 dessertspoon lime juice

½ teaspoon crushed dried chillies

black pepper

2oz/50g vermicelli rice noodles

groundnut oil

Combine the spring onions, garlic, ginger, sesame seeds, sesame oil, soy sauce, lime juice and dried chillies and season with black pepper. Add the tofu and mix thoroughly. Cover and keep in the fridge for 4 hours. Soak the rice noodles in boiling water for 4 minutes, then drain and cut into short lengths and stir into the tofu mixture.

Dip the rice flour pancakes individually into a bowl of hot water for about 20 seconds until pliable, then remove from the water, drain and place on a flat surface. Divide the filling between the 8 pancakes, putting it in the centre. Fold three sides of each pancake over the filling, then roll them up to make small sausage shapes. Shallow fry the rolls in hot groundnut oil for a few minutes on each side until browned, drain on kitchen paper and serve hot with a dressing or a dipping sauce.

Fried battered vegetables with chilli and ginger sauce (serves 4)

1lb/450g prepared vegetables (e.g. cauliflower, broccoli, mushrooms, peppers, courgette), cut into even-sized chunks

groundnut oil

lime wedges

batter

4oz/100g plain flour

5 fl.oz/150ml soya milk

1 tablespoon groundnut oil

½ teaspoon dried crushed chillies

sauce

1 red chilli, deseeded and finely chopped

1 inch/2.5cm piece of root ginger, grated

1 dessertspoon groundnut oil

4 tablespoons rice vinegar

4 tablespoons rice wine

2 tablespoons light soy sauce

2 tablespoons water

1 dessertspoon brown sugar

1 rounded dessertspoon cornflour

Prepare the sauce first. Fry the chilli and ginger in the oil until soft. Remove from the heat, add the remaining sauce ingredients and stir until the cornflour dissolves. Set aside.

Mix the batter ingredients until smooth. Lightly steam the harder vegetables to soften them slightly, then add all the vegetables to the batter mixture and combine until they are coated. Heat some oil in a wok until hot, spoon the individual coated vegetables into the pan and fry until golden.

Meanwhile stir the sauce again, bring to the boil while stirring and continue stirring for a minute or so until it thickens, then pour into to a small bowl. Drain the vegetables on kitchen paper and arrange them on a serving plate with the bowl of sauce in the middle. Garnish the plate with lime wedges.

Stuffed pepper cups (serves 6)

3 peppers, each approx. 4oz/100g

filling

4oz/100g long grain rice

¼oz/7g dried mushrooms

2 shallots, peeled and finely chopped

2 garlic cloves, crushed

2 tablespoons finely chopped fresh coriander

1 tablespoon rice wine

1 dessertspoon groundnut oil

10 fl.oz/300ml boiling water

1 dried bird's-eye chilli, crushed

black pepper

Soak the mushrooms in the boiling water for 1 hour. Cut the peppers in half widthways to make 6 'cups'. Cut off the stalks and remove the membranes and seeds. Fry the shallots and garlic in the oil for 2 minutes. Add the rice and stir around for 30 seconds, then put in the soaked mushrooms and soaking liquid, coriander, rice wine and chilli, and season with black pepper. Stir well, bring to the boil, cover and simmer gently until the liquid has been absorbed and the rice is done. Meanwhile steam the pepper 'cups' until just tender. Transfer to a serving dish and divide the filling equally between them. Spoon a dressing or a dipping sauce over the top before serving.

Peanut, potato and tofu patties (makes 16)

1lb/450g potatoes, peeled

4oz/100g marinated tofu, mashed

3oz/75g roasted peanuts, ground

2 shallots, peeled and grated

groundnut oil

Steam the potatoes, mash and add the tofu, shallots and half of the ground peanuts. Mix thoroughly, then take heaped dessertspoonfuls and roll into balls. Roll these in the remaining ground peanuts, flatten each ball slightly and put on an oiled baking tray. Brush the tops with oil and place under a hot grill until golden brown. Carefully turn the patties over and again brush with oil. Put back under the grill to brown, then serve warm with a dressing or a dipping sauce.

Vegetable and tofu satay (serves 4)

12oz/350g mixed prepared vegetables (e.g. courgette, mushrooms, peppers, tomatoes), cut into even-sized chunks

4oz/100g firm plain tofu, diced

satay sauce (see page 104)

marinade

1 tablespoon groundnut oil

1 tablespoon light soy sauce

1 teaspoon lime juice

1 rounded teaspoon lemon grass purée

1 garlic clove, crushed

black pepper

Mix the marinade ingredients and add to the vegetables and tofu in a large bowl. Combine well, cover and leave to marinate for 2 hours. Make the satay sauce up to the cooking stage.

Thread the vegetables and tofu onto 8 small square skewers and put under a hot grill, turning occasionally, until just tender. Meanwhile heat the satay sauce, stir until it thickens, then transfer to a serving bowl. Arrange the skewers on a plate and serve with the sauce.

Steamed mushroom and rice rolls with chilli and garlic sauce (makes 8)

8 rice flour pancakes

cabbage leaves

filling

2oz/50g long grain rice

4 shallots, peeled and finely chopped

1 garlic clove, crushed

½ red chilli, finely chopped

1 tablespoon groundnut oil

¼oz/7g dried mushrooms

7 fl.oz/200ml boiling water

1 rounded tablespoon finely chopped fresh coriander

1 teaspoon dark soy sauce

black pepper

sauce

1 red chilli, chopped

3 garlic cloves, chopped

2 tablespoons light soy sauce

2 tablespoon lime juice

1 dessertspoon brown sugar

1 dessertspoon water

black pepper

Break the dried mushrooms into tiny pieces and put in the boiling water. Cover and leave to soak for 20 minutes. Fry the shallots, garlic and chilli in the oil until soft, add the rice and stir around for 1 minute. Now add the mushrooms and their soaking water, and the coriander and soy sauce. Season with black pepper and stir well. Bring to the boil, cover and simmer gently until the liquid has been absorbed, then remove from the heat and allow to cool.

Dip each of the rice flour pancakes into a bowl of hot water for about 20 seconds until pliable, remove from the water, drain and spread on a flat surface. Divide the filling equally between the pancakes, putting it in the centre. Fold three sides of each pancake over the filling and roll them up to make small sausage shapes. Line a steamer with a thin layer of cabbage leaves to prevent the pancakes getting stuck to it and place the rice rolls on top. Steam for 5-8 minutes until heated through.

Meanwhile, put the sauce ingredients into a small blender and blend until smooth. Spoon the sauce over the warm rice rolls when serving.

RICE

Rice is the mainstay of the Thai diet and Thailand is reported to be the largest exporter of rice in the world. Many different types are grown, but the most highly prized is Thai jasmine rice, a fragrant long grained variety. In the north of the country short grained glutinous rice is preferred and this is served steamed. Plainly cooked rice of all types is the perfect foil for hot spicy dishes, while flavoured rice dishes mixed with other ingredients are ideal for serving with snacks, salads or flat breads. Leftover rice is never wasted and is used to make other dishes such as congee, a favourite at breakfast, or rice cakes, which are a popular snack food.

Curried sweet pepper rice (serves 4)

10oz/300g mixed peppers, thinly sliced

8oz/225g long grain brown rice

2 shallots, peeled and finely chopped

2 garlic cloves, crushed

1 inch/2.5cm piece of root ginger, finely chopped

1 rounded dessertspoon yellow curry paste (see page 69)

4 cardamom pods, husked and the seeds separated

black pepper

2 tablespoons groundnut oil

chopped fresh coriander

crispy fried shallots (see page 102)

Cook the rice, spread it out in a shallow dish, cover and chill for a couple of hours. Heat the oil in a wok and stir-fry the peppers, shallots, garlic and ginger for 5 minutes, then add the curry paste, cardamom seeds and rice and stir-fry for another 3 minutes. Season with black pepper and transfer to a serving dish. Garnish with chopped coriander and crispy fried shallots.

Coconut rice (serves 4)

8oz/225g long grain white rice

1oz/25g creamed coconut, grated

16 fl.oz/475ml hot water

toasted flaked coconut

Wash the rice in several changes of water and put it in a heavy-based pan. Dissolve the creamed coconut in the hot water and add, stir well and bring to the boil. Cover and simmer very gently for about 15 minutes until the liquid has been absorbed. Remove from the heat and allow to stand for 5 minutes, before fluffing up and transferring to a dish. Garnish with toasted flaked coconut when serving.

Vegetable and peanut fried rice (serves 4)

8oz/225g long grain white rice

2oz/50g green beans, topped, tailed and sliced diagonally

2oz/50g sweetcorn kernels

2oz/50g red pepper, thinly sliced

2oz/50g carrot, scraped and thinly sliced

2oz/50g shelled peas

1 green chilli, finely chopped

1 onion, peeled and finely chopped

2 garlic cloves, crushed

2 tablespoons groundnut oil

2 tablespoons light soy sauce

1½oz/40g roasted peanuts, roughly chopped

lime wedges

fresh coriander leaves

Cook the rice, then spread it out in a shallow dish, cover and chill for a couple of hours. Heat the oil in a wok and stir-fry the green beans, sweetcorn, red pepper, carrot, peas, chilli, onion and garlic for 5 minutes. Add the cooked rice and soy sauce and stir-fry for 3 minutes more. Stir in two-thirds of the peanuts and spoon into a serving bowl. Garnish with the remaining peanuts and with lime wedges and coriander leaves.

Mushroom and coriander rice (serves 4)

8oz/225g long grain white rice

6oz/175g mixed mushrooms, wiped and chopped

½oz/15g dried mushrooms, broken into small pieces

16 fl.oz/475ml boiling water

1 red chilli, finely chopped

4 shallots, peeled and finely chopped

2 garlic cloves, crushed

4 rounded tablespoons finely chopped fresh coriander

2 tablespoons groundnut oil

1 tablespoon dark soy sauce

black pepper

extra coriander leaves

Soak the dried mushrooms in a saucepan in the boiling water for 20 minutes, then add the rice and bring to the boil. Cover and simmer gently until the liquid has been absorbed. Allow to cool, spread the rice out in a shallow dish, cover and refrigerate until cold.

Stir-fry the chilli, shallots and garlic in the oil for 3 minutes. Add the mushrooms and chopped coriander and stir until the juices begin to run. Now add the cooked rice and the soy sauce and season with black pepper. Continue stir-frying for 3 minutes, then transfer to a dish and serve garnished with coriander leaves.

Fragrant Thai and baby corn rice (serves 4)

8oz/225g Thai jasmine rice

8oz/225g baby corn cobs, cut into ¼ inch/5mm diagonal slices

1 shallot, peeled and finely chopped

1 garlic clove, crushed

1 lemon grass stalk, finely chopped

2 tablespoons groundnut oil

black pepper

chopped fresh mint leaves

Cook the rice and spread it out in a shallow dish. Cover and chill for a couple of hours. Heat the oil in a wok and stir-fry the baby corn, shallot, garlic and lemon grass for 5 minutes, add the rice and season with black pepper and stir-fry for 3 minutes more. Spoon into a serving dish and garnish with chopped mint.

Stir-fried beansprouts with brown rice and cashews (serves 4)

8oz/225g beansprouts

8oz/225g long grain brown rice

2oz/50g roasted cashew nuts, halved

6 spring onions, trimmed and sliced

1 inch/2.5cm piece of root ginger, finely chopped

2 garlic cloves, crushed

1 red chilli, finely chopped

1 tablespoon groundnut oil

1 tablespoon sesame oil

black pepper

Cook the rice, then spread it out in a shallow dish, cover and put in the fridge for a couple of hours. Stir-fry the spring onions, ginger, garlic and chilli in the groundnut oil for 3 minutes. Add the beansprouts and fry for 1 minute. Mix the sesame oil with the cooked rice and add to the pan, season with black pepper and continue stir-frying for another 3 minutes. Stir in two-thirds of the cashew nuts, transfer the rice to a dish and garnish with the remaining nuts.

Pineapple jasmine rice (serves 4)

8oz/225g Thai jasmine rice

8oz/225g tin pineapple slices in natural juice

1 dessertspoon groundnut oil

2 shallots, peeled and finely chopped

1 small red chilli, finely chopped

1 rounded dessertspoon lemon grass purée

1 dessertspoon light soy sauce

2 kaffir lime leaves

14 fl.oz/425ml vegetable stock

finely sliced spring onions

fresh basil leaves

Wash the rice in several changes of water and allow to drain. Heat the oil and gently fry the shallots and chilli until soft, then stir in the rice together with the juice from the pineapple. Chop the pineapple slices and add to the pan, together with the lemon grass purée, soy sauce, vegetable stock and lime leaves. Combine well and bring to the boil. Lower the heat, cover and simmer very gently for about 15 minutes until the liquid has been absorbed. Put into a serving dish and garnish with spring onion slices and fresh basil leaves.

Yellow rice (serves 4)

8oz/225g long grain white rice

6oz/175g yellow pepper, sliced

6oz/175g tinned bamboo shoots, drained and sliced

2 shallots, peeled and chopped

1 garlic clove, crushed

2 tablespoons groundnut oil

1 rounded dessertspoon lemon grass purée

1 teaspoon turmeric

black pepper

cucumber slices

crispy fried shallots (see page 102)

Cook the rice until tender, spread it out in a shallow dish, cover and chill for two hours. Heat the oil in a wok and stir-fry the yellow pepper, shallots and garlic for 3 minutes, then add the turmeric and lemon grass and stir until combined. Now put in the rice and bamboo shoots and season with black pepper. Continue stir-frying for a further 3 minutes, transfer to a dish and garnish with cucumber slices and crispy fried shallots.

Broad bean and chilli rice (serves 4)

8oz/225g Thai jasmine rice

12oz/350g shelled broad beans

4 shallots, peeled and finely chopped

2 green chillies, finely chopped

2 garlic cloves, crushed

1 inch/2.5cm piece of root ginger, grated

2 tablespoons groundnut oil

1 tablespoon light soy sauce

black pepper

shredded fresh basil leaves

Cook the rice and keep it in the fridge for a couple of hours, spread out in a covered shallow dish. Steam the broad beans until tender, rinse them under cold running water and remove the skins. Heat the oil in a wok and stir-fry the shallots, chillies, garlic and ginger until soft. Add the cooked rice, broad beans and soy sauce, season with black pepper and stir-fry for 3 minutes more. Spoon into a dish and garnish with shredded basil leaves.

Carrot, ginger and sesame fried rice (serves 4)

1lb/450g carrots, scraped and cut into ½ inch/1cm matchsticks

8oz/225g long grain brown rice

2 inch/5cm piece of root ginger, grated

1 red chilli, finely chopped

2 tablespoons groundnut oil

1 tablespoon light soy sauce

1 teaspoon turmeric

1 tablespoon sesame oil

roasted sesame seeds

Cook the rice, spread it out in a shallow dish, cover and refrigerate until cold. Stir-fry the carrot, ginger and chilli in the groundnut oil until just tender. Mix the soy sauce, turmeric and sesame oil with the rice and add to the pan. Continue stir-frying for 2-3 minutes. Serve sprinkled with roasted sesame seeds.

Rice cakes (makes approx. 30)

8oz/225g short grain glutinous rice

groundnut oil

Steam the rice until tender, then allow to cool. Take rounded dessertspoonfuls and shape into small patties. Shallow fry the rice cakes in hot groundnut oil for a few minutes on each side until golden. Drain on kitchen paper and serve hot with a sauce or dressing.

Rice and corn congee (serves 4)

8oz/225g long grain white rice

8oz/225g sweetcorn kernels

4 shallots, peeled and finely chopped

2 garlic cloves, crushed

1 inch/2.5cm piece of root ginger, grated

½ teaspoon crushed dried chilli

1 tablespoon groundnut oil

24 fl.oz/725ml vegetable stock

1 tablespoon light soy sauce

2 rounded tablespoons finely chopped fresh coriander

black pepper

extra chopped fresh coriander

Cook the rice, drain and set aside. Fry the shallots, garlic and ginger in the oil until softened. Add the cooked rice and the remaining ingredients apart from the extra coriander, and bring to the boil. Cover and simmer gently for about 15 minutes, stirring occasionally, until the mixture thickens. Spoon into serving bowls and garnish with fresh coriander.

NOODLES

Noodles, which are believed to have been introduced to Thailand by early Chinese settlers, now rate as the country's second most important food. Taking only minutes to prepare, this is the ultimate fast food and noodles are enjoyed at any time of the day, either freshly prepared at home or bought from street vendors. Noodles can be served plain as a simple accompaniment or they can form the basis of more substantial dishes when added to other ingredients. Some of the more frequently used noodles are made from rice, wheat and mung beans, although other types are easily available. Luckily for vegans, many of them do not contain eggs.

Stir-fried vegetables with rice noodles and cashews (serves 4)

4oz/100g flat rice noodles

4oz/100g courgette, cut into thin ribbon strips

4oz/100g carrot, scraped and cut into thin ribbon strips

4oz/100g red pepper, thinly sliced

2oz/50g mushrooms, wiped and sliced

1 celery stick, trimmed and finely sliced

1 onion, peeled and finely sliced

2 garlic cloves, crushed

½ red chilli, finely chopped

½ inch/1cm piece of root ginger, finely chopped

2 tablespoons groundnut oil

1oz/25g roasted cashew nuts, roughly chopped

1 tablespoon light soy sauce

1 dessertspoon lime juice

black pepper

finely sliced spring onions

fresh coriander leaves

Soak the noodles in boiling water for 4 minutes. Drain and rinse in cold water, then cut into shorter lengths and set aside. Heat the oil in a wok and stir-fry the celery, onion, garlic, chilli and ginger for 3 minutes. Add the courgette, carrot, red pepper and mushrooms and stir-fry for another 5 minutes. Put in the drained noodles together with the soy sauce and lime juice, season with black pepper and continue stir-frying for 2-3 minutes. Remove from the heat and stir in the cashews. Garnish with spring onions and coriander when serving.

Green noodles with broccoli, mushrooms and tomatoes (serves 4)

14oz/400g tin straw mushrooms, drained and rinsed

8oz/225g broccoli, chopped

8oz/225g tomatoes, skinned and chopped

4oz/100g spinach noodles

1 tablespoon groundnut oil

4 shallots, peeled and finely chopped

1 inch/2.5cm piece of root ginger, finely chopped

2 fl.oz/50ml water

3 garlic cloves, crushed

1 tablespoon light soy sauce

1 tablespoon rice vinegar

1 teaspoon brown sugar

2 dried bird's-eye chillies, crushed

black pepper

finely sliced spring onions

quartered cherry tomatoes

Mix the tomatoes with the garlic, soy sauce, vinegar, sugar, chillies and water and season with black pepper. Heat the oil in a wok and stir-fry the shallots and ginger for 2 minutes. Add the broccoli and the tomato mixture and cook, stirring frequently, for about 10 minutes until almost tender. Meanwhile, soak the noodles in boiling water for 5 minutes. Drain and cut into shorter lengths, then add to the wok together with the mushrooms. Continue stirring for a couple of minutes until well combined. Transfer to a serving bowl and garnish with spring onions and cherry tomatoes.

Rice vermicelli with soya mince and peas (serves 4)

6oz/175g rice vermicelli

3oz/75g natural minced textured vegetable protein

15 fl.oz/450ml hot vegetable stock

1 rounded tablespoon tamarind purée

2 rounded tablespoons red curry paste (see page 68)

6oz/175g shelled peas

1 red onion, peeled and finely chopped

2 garlic cloves, crushed

1 tablespoon groundnut oil

4 fl.oz/125ml coconut milk

4 rounded tablespoons finely chopped fresh coriander

black pepper

1 red chilli, deseeded and finely chopped

crushed roasted peanuts

Dissolve the tamarind purée in the vegetable stock, stir in the vegetable protein, cover and leave for 1 hour. Fry the onion and garlic in the oil until softened. Add the red curry paste and stir around for 1 minute, then stir in the soaked vegetable protein and remaining stock, peas, coconut milk and coriander. Season with black pepper and bring to the boil. Simmer, stirring occasionally, for 5 minutes.

Meanwhile soak the rice vermicelli in boiling water for 3 minutes. Drain and cut into smaller pieces and add to the pan. Combine well and continue cooking for another couple of minutes. Spoon into a warmed bowl and serve garnished with the chopped chilli and the crushed peanuts.

Wheat noodles with mushrooms (serves 4)

8oz/225g wheat noodles

8oz/225g mushrooms, wiped and sliced

½oz/15g dried mushrooms, finely chopped

4 fl.oz/125ml boiling water

1 tablespoon soy sauce

1 tablespoon rice wine

2 tablespoons groundnut oil

4 shallots, peeled and finely chopped

2 garlic cloves, crushed

1 red chilli, finely chopped

4 rounded tablespoons finely chopped fresh coriander

black pepper

chopped roasted cashew nuts

Put the dried mushrooms in a bowl with the 4 fl.oz/125ml boiling water, cover and leave for an hour. Soak the noodles in a pan of boiling water for 4 minutes, drain and cut into short lengths. Heat the oil in a wok and stir-fry the shallots, garlic and chilli for 3 minutes. Add the soaked mushrooms and remaining liquid, fresh mushrooms, soy sauce, rice wine and coriander and season with black pepper. Cook whilst stirring for 2 minutes, then add the noodles and cook for 2 minutes more until heated through. Garnish with chopped cashew nuts.

Sesame fried noodles with beansprouts (serves 4)

8oz/225g beansprouts

4oz/100g flat rice noodles

4 shallots, peeled and finely chopped

1 red chilli, finely chopped

2 garlic cloves, crushed

½oz/15g roasted sesame seeds

1 tablespoon sesame oil

1 tablespoon groundnut oil

1 tablespoon lime juice

1 tablespoon light soy sauce

black pepper

finely chopped fresh root ginger

Soak the rice noodles in boiling water for 4 minutes, drain and rinse under cold running water and cut into shorter lengths. Stir-fry the shallots, chilli and garlic in the groundnut oil for 3 minutes. Add the beansprouts and fry for 1 minute, then add the sesame oil, noodles, sesame seeds, lime juice and soy sauce. Season with black pepper and stir-fry for a further 2-3 minutes. Sprinkle with finely chopped root ginger before serving.

Marinated courgettes with green noodles (serves 4/6)

1½lb/675g courgettes, halved lengthways and sliced

8oz/225g spinach noodles

finely sliced spring onions

marinade

4 shallots, peeled and chopped

2 green chillies, deseeded and chopped

2 garlic cloves, chopped

4 rounded tablespoons chopped fresh coriander

2 dessertspoons dark soy sauce

2 rounded dessertspoons lemon grass purée

2 dessertspoons groundnut oil

1 tablespoon lime juice

black pepper

Put the marinade ingredients in a small blender and blend until smooth. Add to the courgettes and mix thoroughly. Cover and chill for 2 hours. Transfer the marinated courgettes to a pan and cook, stirring occasionally, until just tender. Meanwhile, soak the noodles in boiling water for 5 minutes. Drain and add to the cooked courgettes, toss well and put into a serving dish. Sprinkle with finely sliced spring onions.

Sweet and sour wheat noodles with pineapple and vegetables (serves 4)

8oz/225g tin pineapple in natural juice, drained and chopped

4oz/100g wheat noodles

4oz/100g white cabbage, finely shredded

4oz/100g carrots, scraped and cut into matchsticks

4oz/100g green pepper, sliced

2oz/50g mushrooms, wiped and sliced

1 celery stick, trimmed and finely sliced

4 shallots, peeled and finely chopped

2 garlic cloves, crushed

1 inch/2.5cm piece of root ginger, finely chopped

1 red chilli, finely chopped

2 tablespoons groundnut oil

2 tablespoons rice vinegar

1 tablespoon light soy sauce

1 dessertspoon brown sugar

1 dessertspoon lemon grass purée

4 cucumber slices, chopped

roasted cashew nuts

Heat the oil in a wok and stir-fry the cabbage, carrots, green pepper, mushrooms, celery, shallots, garlic, ginger and chilli until just done. Meanwhile soak the noodles in boiling water for 4 minutes, drain and cut into short lengths. Mix the vinegar with the soy sauce, sugar and lemon grass purée and add to the pan together with the noodles and pineapple. Continue stir-frying for a couple of minutes, then serve garnished with chopped cucumber and cashew nuts.

Rice noodles with pepper, peanut and coconut sauce (serves 4)

4oz/100g thin rice noodles

12oz/350g mixed peppers, sliced

2oz/50g roasted peanuts, ground

4 shallots, peeled and finely chopped

2 garlic cloves, crushed

1 red chilli, finely chopped

½oz/15g creamed coconut, grated

8 fl.oz/225ml vegetable stock

1 tablespoon lime juice

1 tablespoon groundnut oil

1 tablespoon light soy sauce

1 rounded teaspoon brown sugar

black pepper

shredded fresh basil leaves

Stir-fry the peppers, shallots, garlic and chilli in the oil until just tender. Soak the noodles in boiling water for 4 minutes, then drain and cut into shorter lengths. Add the peanuts, coconut, stock, lime juice, soy sauce and sugar to the peppers and season with black pepper. Stir well and bring to the boil. Continue stirring for a minute or so until the sauce thickens, then remove from the heat and add the drained noodles. Mix well and garnish with shredded basil leaves to serve.

Mixed green vegetables with spinach noodles (serves 4)

8oz/225g courgette, quartered lengthways and cut into diagonal slices

6oz/175g kale

6oz/175g green pepper, chopped

4oz/100g spinach noodles

4 shallots, peeled and finely chopped

1 green chilli, finely chopped

1 lemon grass stalk, finely chopped

1 tablespoon groundnut oil

1 rounded tablespoon coriander and garlic dressing (see page 103)

10 fl.oz/300ml vegetable stock or water

1 tablespoon light soy sauce

1 tablespoon lime juice

1 teaspoon brown sugar

4 kaffir lime leaves

black pepper

chopped roasted peanuts

Cut the thick stalks from the kale and finely shred the leaves. Heat the oil in a wok and stir-fry the shallots, chilli and lemon grass for 3 minutes. Put in the courgette and green pepper and stir-fry for 2 minutes, then add the kale and fry for 3 minutes more. Break the noodles into small pieces and add to the pan. Mix the coriander and garlic dressing, soy sauce, lime juice and sugar with the stock and add together with the lime leaves. Season with black pepper, stir well and bring to the boil. Simmer, stirring frequently, for about 5 minutes, until the liquid has been absorbed and the noodles and vegetables are done. Spoon into a serving dish and garnish with chopped peanuts.

Chilli noodles with tofu and peppers (serves 4)

4oz/100g chilli-flavoured noodles

8oz/225g firm tofu, finely diced

8oz/225g mixed peppers, chopped

2 shallots, peeled and sliced

1 red chilli

1 tablespoon groundnut oil

1 tablespoon tamarind purée

1 tablespoon light soy sauce

1 tablespoon rice vinegar

1 rounded teaspoon brown sugar

2 garlic cloves, crushed

chopped fresh coriander

Put the tofu in a small bowl, combine the tamarind purée with the soy sauce, vinegar, sugar and garlic and add. Mix thoroughly, cover and chill for a couple of hours. Cut a few thin rings from the chilli and keep for garnish. Finely chop the rest and stir-fry with the shallots and peppers in the oil until almost tender. Meanwhile soak the noodles in boiling water for 4 minutes, then drain and add to the pan together with the tofu. Continue stir-frying for a couple of minutes, transfer to a serving dish and garnish with the chilli rings and some chopped coriander.

Aubergine and tomatoes with rice vermicelli (serves 4)

1lb/450g aubergine, finely diced

6oz/175g tomatoes, skinned and chopped

4oz/100g rice vermicelli

4 shallots, peeled and finely chopped

2 garlic cloves, crushed

1 inch/2.5cm piece of root ginger, finely chopped

3 tablespoons groundnut oil

1 tablespoon tamarind purée

1 tablespoon rice wine

1 tablespoon rice vinegar

4 kaffir lime leaves

2 dried bird's-eye chillies, crushed

black pepper

chopped roasted cashew nuts

Stir-fry the aubergine, shallots, garlic and ginger in the oil for 10 minutes. Mix the tomatoes with the tamarind purée, rice wine, rice vinegar, lime leaves and chillies and season with black pepper. Add to the pan and continue cooking for 10 minutes. Meanwhile, soak the vermicelli in boiling water for 4 minutes, drain and cut into shorter lengths. Add to the vegetables and combine well. Sprinkle with cashew nuts and serve.

Cellophane noodles with tomatoes and tofu (serves 4)

6oz/175g cellophane noodles

8oz/225g tomatoes, skinned and finely chopped

4oz/100g plain tofu, finely diced

3 shallots, peeled and finely chopped

1 celery stick, trimmed and finely chopped

1 inch/2.5cm piece of galangal, chopped

1 tablespoon groundnut oil

1 tablespoon light soy sauce

1 tablespoon rice vinegar

2 garlic cloves, crushed

2 dried bird's-eye chillies, crushed

black pepper

chopped roasted peanuts

Put the tomatoes, tofu, soy sauce, vinegar, garlic and chillies in a bowl and season with black pepper, mix well, cover and refrigerate for 1 hour. Heat the oil in a wok and fry the shallots, celery and galangal until cooked. Meanwhile soak the noodles in boiling water for 4 minutes, then drain and cut into short lengths. Add the noodles to the wok together with the tomato and tofu mixture and continue stir-frying for 2-3 minutes. Transfer to a serving dish and garnish with chopped peanuts.

Rice stick noodles with stir-fried pak-choi and coriander (serves 4)

8oz/225g pak-choi, finely shredded

4oz/100g thin rice stick noodles

4 shallots, peeled and finely chopped

1 green chilli, finely chopped

1 tablespoon groundnut oil

2 tablespoons coriander and garlic dressing (see page 103)

black pepper

crispy fried garlic (see page 102)

Heat the oil in a wok and stir-fry the shallots and chilli for 2 minutes, then add the pak-choi and stir-fry until almost tender. Meanwhile, soak the noodles in boiling water for 4 minutes. Drain and cut into smaller pieces. Add to the wok together with the coriander and garlic dressing, season with black pepper and continue stir-frying for a couple of minutes until well combined. Serve garnished with crispy fried garlic.

CURRY PASTES AND CURRIES

Thai cooks traditionally make their own favourite curry pastes from handed-down recipes, by carefully and painstakingly blending the ingredients in a mortar with a pestle. A small blender is ideal for cooks with less time to spare and any unused paste can be stored in an airtight jar in the fridge for up to two weeks. Once you've made the paste, distinctively flavoured Thai curries are quick and easy to prepare. They are generally served as part of the main meal with complementing dishes and large bowls of steamed rice.

Green curry paste

2oz/50g green chillies, deseeded and chopped

2 lemon grass stalks, chopped

1 inch/2.5cm piece of root ginger, chopped

2 shallots, peeled and chopped

4 garlic cloves, chopped

2 rounded tablespoons finely chopped coriander leaves and root

1 dessertspoon lime juice

2 dessertspoons groundnut oil

1 dessertspoon coriander seeds

1 dessertspoon cumin seeds

black pepper

Dry-fry the coriander and cumin seeds, then grind them in a mortar with a pestle. Mix with the remaining ingredients and blend to a paste.

Red curry paste

2oz/50g red chillies, deseeded and chopped

1 lemon grass stalk, chopped

1 inch/2.5cm piece of galangal, chopped

1 small red onion, peeled and chopped

2 garlic cloves, chopped

1 dessertspoon coriander seeds

1 dessertspoon cumin seeds

1 tablespoon chopped coriander root

1 teaspoon lime juice

1 teaspoon grated lime peel

½ teaspoon turmeric

2 dessertspoons groundnut oil

black pepper

Dry-fry the coriander and cumin seeds. Grind them in a mortar with a pestle, then mix with the rest of the ingredients and blend to a paste.

Yellow curry paste

2oz/50g yellow chillies, deseeded and chopped

1 lemon grass stalk, chopped

1 inch/2.5cm piece of root ginger, chopped

2 shallots, peeled and chopped

2 garlic cloves, chopped

1 rounded dessertspoon coriander seeds

1 teaspoon turmeric

2 dessertspoons groundnut oil

black pepper

Dry-fry the coriander seeds and grind them in a mortar with a pestle. Combine with the remaining ingredients and blend to a paste.

Mussaman curry paste

2oz/50g red chillies, deseeded and chopped

1 lemon grass stalk, chopped

1 shallot, peeled and chopped

2 garlic cloves, chopped

1 inch/2.5cm piece of root ginger, chopped

1 teaspoon cumin seeds

1 teaspoon coriander seeds

2 cardamom pods, husked and the seeds separated

¼ teaspoon ground cinnamon

¼ teaspoon ground cloves

1 dessertspoon lime juice

2 dessertspoons groundnut oil

black pepper

Dry-fry the cumin, coriander and cardamom seeds and, using a pestle, grind them in a mortar. Blend to a paste with the other ingredients.

Sweet potato and pineapple curry (serves 4/6)

1½lb/675g sweet potato, peeled and diced

14oz/400g tin pineapple in natural juice

6 shallots, peeled and finely chopped

3 garlic cloves, crushed

2 inch/5cm piece of galangal, finely chopped

2 rounded tablespoons yellow curry paste

1 rounded dessertspoon lemon grass purée

4 kaffir lime leaves

1 tablespoon groundnut oil

4 fl.oz/125ml water

1 teaspoon turmeric

black pepper

1oz/25g creamed coconut, grated

chopped roasted cashew nuts

Fry the shallots, garlic and galangal in the oil until soft. Add the curry paste, lemon grass purée and turmeric and stir around for 1 minute. Strain the juice from the pineapple and add the juice, sweet potato, lime leaves and water to the pan, season with black pepper and stir well. Bring to the boil, then cover and simmer gently, stirring occasionally, for about 25 minutes until the potato is done. Chop the pineapple and add, together with the creamed coconut. Continue stirring for a minute or so until the coconut dissolves. Garnish with chopped cashew nuts before serving.

Green vegetable curry (serves 4/6)

1lb/450g courgette, halved lengthways and cut into diagonal
slices

8oz/225g green beans, topped, tailed and cut into diagonal slices

8oz/225g green pepper, thinly sliced

1 onion, peeled and chopped

2 garlic cloves, crushed

2 tablespoons green curry paste

4 tablespoons finely chopped fresh coriander

1 tablespoon groundnut oil

1 dessertspoon lime juice

6 fl.oz/175ml vegetable stock or water

4 fl.oz/125ml coconut milk

fresh basil leaves

Heat the oil and fry the onion and garlic until softened. Add the curry paste and stir around for 1 minute, then the courgette, green beans, green pepper, stock and coriander and combine well. Raise the heat and simmer for 5 minutes. Add the lime juice and coconut milk and continue simmering, stirring occasionally, for about 10 minutes until the vegetables are tender. Serve garnished with fresh basil leaves.

Broccoli and tomato curry (serves 4/6)

1lb/450g broccoli, chopped

12oz/350g tomatoes, skinned and chopped

6 shallots, peeled and finely chopped

2 garlic cloves, crushed

1 tablespoon groundnut oil

2 rounded tablespoons green curry paste

8 kaffir lime leaves

1 teaspoon turmeric

8 fl.oz/225ml thin coconut milk

1 red chilli, cut into thin rings

toasted cashew nuts

Fry the shallots and garlic in the oil for 2 minutes. Add the tomatoes, curry paste, lime leaves and turmeric and cook for another 2 minutes. Stir in the coconut milk and broccoli and simmer gently, stirring occasionally, until cooked. Transfer to a serving dish and garnish with red chilli rings and cashew nuts.

Curried aubergine with tofu (serves 4/6)

1lb/450g aubergine, finely diced

6oz/175g firm tofu, finely diced

6oz/175g tomatoes, skinned and chopped

1 red onion, peeled and finely chopped

3 garlic cloves, crushed

3 tablespoons groundnut oil

2 rounded tablespoons red curry paste

1 teaspoon turmeric

black pepper

1 rounded dessertspoon tamarind purée

1oz/25g creamed coconut

6 fl.oz/175ml boiling water

shredded fresh basil leaves

Heat the oil and fry the aubergine, onion and garlic for 10 minutes while stirring frequently. Add the tomatoes, curry paste, turmeric and tamarind and stir around for 2 minutes. Dissolve the creamed coconut in the water and add to the pan, together with the tofu. Season with black pepper and simmer gently for 10 minutes, stirring regularly until done. Garnish with shredded fresh basil when serving.

Peanut and pumpkin curry (serves 4/6)

2lb/900g firm pumpkin flesh, diced

4oz/100g roasted peanuts, ground

6 shallots, peeled and finely chopped

2 garlic cloves, crushed

1 inch/2.5cm piece of root ginger, finely chopped

1 tablespoon groundnut oil

2 rounded tablespoons red curry paste

2 rounded tablespoons finely chopped fresh coriander

14 fl.oz/425ml thin coconut milk

chopped roasted peanuts

chopped red chilli

Fry the shallots, garlic and ginger for 2 minutes in the oil. Add the curry paste and stir around for 1 minute, then put in the pumpkin, coriander and coconut milk and stir well. Raise the heat and simmer for about 20 minutes until tender. Add the ground peanuts and while stirring continue cooking for a minute or two. Spoon into a serving dish and garnish with chopped peanuts and chilli.

Aubergine and cashew nut curry (serves 4/6)

1½lb/675g aubergine, diced

8oz/225g red pepper, chopped

1 red onion, peeled and finely chopped

1½ inch/3cm piece of root ginger, finely chopped

4oz/100g roasted cashew nuts

3 rounded tablespoons red curry paste

4 tablespoons groundnut oil

4 fl.oz/125ml vegetable stock or water

4 fl.oz/125ml thin coconut milk

6 kaffir lime leaves

black pepper

fresh basil leaves

Heat the oil and fry the aubergine, onion and ginger for 10 minutes, stirring frequently. Add the red pepper, curry paste, vegetable stock, coconut milk and lime leaves and combine well. Raise the heat and simmer for 15 minutes, stirring frequently. Keep ½oz/15g of the cashew nuts, grind the rest and add to the curry. Season with black pepper. Continue simmering for a couple of minutes, stirring constantly, then transfer to a dish and garnish with the remaining cashew nuts and with fresh basil leaves.

Yellow vegetable curry (serves 4/6)

1lb/450g firm pumpkin flesh, diced

12oz/350g yellow or green courgette, halved lengthways and sliced

8oz/225g yellow pepper, sliced

6 shallots, peeled and finely chopped

4 garlic cloves, crushed

1 inch/2.5cm piece of galangal, finely chopped

2oz/50g crushed roasted peanuts

2 rounded tablespoons yellow curry paste

1 tablespoon groundnut oil

6 kaffir lime leaves

black pepper

8 fl.oz/225ml vegetable stock

6 fl.oz/175ml coconut milk

yellow chilli rings

shredded fresh basil leaves

Soften the shallots, garlic and galangal in the oil. Put in the curry paste and stir around for one minute. Add the pumpkin, stock and lime leaves and season with black pepper. Raise the heat and simmer for 3 minutes, then stir in the courgette, yellow pepper and coconut milk and continue simmering, stirring frequently, for 5-10 minutes until the vegetables are cooked. Stir in the peanuts and garnish with chilli rings and shredded basil leaves.

Mussaman potato and carrot curry
(serves 4/6)

1½lb/675g potatoes, peeled and diced

1½lb/675g carrots, scraped and diced

2oz/50g roasted peanuts, finely chopped

1 onion, peeled and chopped

2 rounded tablespoons mussaman curry paste

1 tablespoon groundnut oil

1 tablespoon tamarind purée

12 fl.oz/350ml vegetable stock

8 fl.oz/225ml coconut milk

6 kaffir lime leaves

1 inch/2.5cm stick of cinnamon

8 cardamom pods, husked and the seeds separated

black pepper

red chilli rings

Heat the oil and fry the onion until softened. Add the curry paste, potatoes and carrots and stir around for 2 minutes. Dissolve the tamarind purée in the stock and put in the pan with the lime leaves, cinnamon and cardamom seeds. Season with black pepper and stir well, then raise the heat and simmer, stirring occasionally, for 15 minutes. Add the coconut milk and peanuts and continue simmering, again stirring occasionally, for about 20 minutes until the vegetables are tender and the sauce has reduced. Spoon into a serving dish and garnish with red chilli rings.

Mixed vegetable and tofu curry (serves 4/6)

8oz/225g firm tofu, diced

6oz/175g carrot, scraped and cut into matchsticks

4oz/100g white cabbage, shredded

4oz/100g green beans, topped, tailed and cut into ½ inch/1cm
   lengths

4oz/100g red pepper, sliced

4oz/100g cauliflower, cut into tiny florets

2oz/50g baby sweetcorn, cut into diagonal slices

4 shallots, peeled and finely chopped

2 garlic cloves, crushed

1 inch/2.5cm piece of galangal, finely chopped

2 rounded tablespoons mussaman curry paste

1 tablespoon groundnut oil

8 cardamom pods, husked and the seeds separated

4 kaffir lime leaves

½ teaspoon turmeric

black pepper

6 fl.oz/175ml vegetable stock

5 fl.oz/150ml coconut milk

1 dessertspoon cornflour

chopped roasted peanuts

chopped fresh coriander

Fry the shallots, garlic and galangal in the oil for 3 minutes, then add the curry paste and turmeric and stir around for a minute. Now add the carrot, cabbage, green beans, red pepper, cauliflower, baby sweetcorn, cardamom seeds, lime leaves and vegetable stock. Season with black pepper and stir well, bring to the boil, cover and simmer, stirring occasionally, for 15 minutes. Put in the tofu and continue cooking for about 5 minutes until the vegetables are done. Mix the cornflour with the coconut milk until smooth and stir into the curry. Continue cooking for a minute or so until the sauce thickens, then transfer to a warmed dish and garnish with chopped peanuts and fresh coriander.

VEGETABLES

Stir-frying, steaming and braising are all typical methods for cooking Thai-style vegetable dishes and these are traditionally served alongside other dishes and rice as part of the main meal. Depending on the numbers sharing a small or larger selection of vegetables is served and the serving quantities are based on traditional-style meals where diners help themselves to small amounts of lots of different dishes.

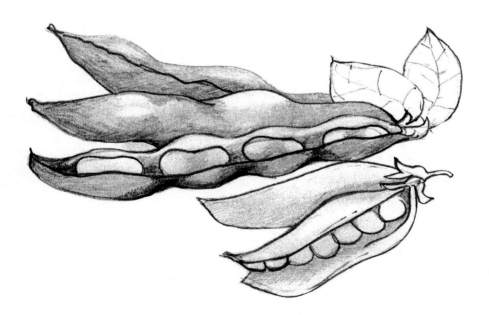

Braised vegetables with coconut (serves 4/6)

1½lb/675g prepared vegetables (e.g. aubergine, courgette, peppers), cut into even-sized diagonal shapes

1-2 red chillies, chopped

2 garlic cloves, chopped

1 lemon grass stalk, chopped

1 inch/2.5cm piece of root ginger, chopped

2 tablespoons groundnut oil

6 fl.oz/175ml vegetable stock

2oz/50g creamed coconut, grated

finely sliced spring onions

Blend the chillies with the garlic, lemon grass and ginger. Heat the oil in a wok and fry this mixture for a couple of minutes. Add the vegetables and stir-fry for 3 minutes, then pour in the stock. Raise the heat and simmer, stirring occasionally, for a few minutes until just tender. Add the coconut and stir until it dissolves. Put in a serving dish and garnish with spring onions.

Hot chilli cabbage (serves 4/6)

1lb/450g white cabbage

2 shallots, peeled and sliced

4oz/100g tomato, skinned and finely chopped

1 teaspoon crushed dried chillies

2 garlic cloves, crushed

2 dessertspoons groundnut oil

1 dessertspoon rice vinegar

1 dessertspoon rice wine

black pepper

red chilli rings

finely chopped fresh coriander

Mix the tomato with the dried chillies, garlic, vinegar and wine and season with black pepper. Remove any thick stalks from the cabbage, then finely shred it and stir-fry it with the shallots in the oil in a wok until nearly cooked. Add the tomato mixture and continue stir-frying for a minute or two until done. Serve garnished with red chilli rings and fresh coriander.

Straw mushrooms with mixed peppers (serves 4/6)

14oz/400g tin straw mushrooms, drained, rinsed and halved

12oz/350g mixed peppers, chopped

4 shallots, peeled and finely chopped

1 red chilli, finely chopped

2 garlic cloves, crushed

1 tablespoon groundnut oil

2 rounded tablespoons finely chopped fresh coriander

1 dessertspoon brown sugar

1 teaspoon lemon grass purée

1 dessertspoon dark soy sauce

black pepper

½oz/15g creamed coconut, grated

finely sliced spring onions

Stir-fry the shallots, chilli and garlic in the oil for 2 minutes. Add the peppers, sugar and lemon grass purée and continue cooking until the peppers are almost tender. Now add the mushrooms, coriander, soy sauce and coconut, season with black pepper and stir for a minute or two until the coconut dissolves. Spoon into a dish and garnish with sliced spring onions.

Stir-fried vegetables with tofu (serves 4/6)

4oz/100g marinated tofu pieces

4oz/100g white cabbage, shredded

4oz/100g green beans, topped, tailed and cut into 1 inch/2.5cm lengths

4oz/100g red pepper, sliced

2oz/50g tinned sliced bamboo shoots, drained

2oz/50g baby sweetcorn, thickly sliced

2oz/50g mushrooms, wiped and sliced

4 shallots, peeled and sliced

1 inch/2.5cm piece of root ginger, finely chopped

1 red chilli, finely chopped

2 garlic cloves, crushed

1 tablespoon groundnut oil

1 dessertspoon sesame oil

1 dessertspoon lemon grass purée

1 dessertspoon light soy sauce

black pepper

roasted sesame seeds

Heat the groundnut oil in a wok and stir-fry the shallots, ginger, chilli, garlic, red pepper, cabbage and green beans until nearly done. Add the remaining ingredients apart from the sesame seeds and continue stir-frying for a couple of minutes until just cooked. Serve garnished with roasted sesame seeds.

Broccoli with peanut and chilli sauce
(serves 4/6)

12oz/350g broccoli, cut into even-sized pieces

2oz/50g roasted peanuts, ground

2 red chillies

2 garlic cloves, crushed

4 shallots, peeled and finely chopped

1 tablespoon groundnut oil

1 tablespoon light soy sauce

1 dessertspoon brown sugar

6 fl.oz/175ml water

black pepper

chopped roasted peanuts

Cut a few thin rings from one of the chillies and keep for garnish. Deseed and finely chop the rest and fry in the oil in a saucepan with the garlic and shallots until soft. Add the ground peanuts, soy sauce, sugar and water and season with black pepper. Stir well, bring to the boil and simmer gently for 3 minutes while stirring, until the sauce thickens. Remove from the heat and keep warm. Steam the broccoli until just tender, then mix into the sauce. Transfer to a serving dish and garnish with chopped peanuts and the chilli rings.

Cauliflower and sesame braise (serves 4/6)

12oz/350g cauliflower, cut into small florets

2 shallots, peeled and finely chopped

2 garlic cloves, crushed

1 small red chilli, deseeded and finely chopped

2 dessertspoons groundnut oil

8 fl.oz/225ml vegetable stock or water

1 dessertspoon dark soy sauce

1 dessertspoon sesame oil

½oz/15g sesame seeds, roasted

Heat the groundnut oil in a wok and stir-fry the shallots, garlic and chilli for 2 minutes. Add the cauliflower and fry for 2 minutes more. Now add the stock and simmer until the cauliflower is just done. Stir in the soy sauce, sesame oil and sesame seeds and serve.

Marinated courgettes with tomato (serves 4/6)

1½lb/675g courgettes, halved lengthways and sliced

4oz/100g tomato, skinned and finely chopped

4 shallots, peeled and chopped

1 green chilli, deseeded and chopped

2 garlic cloves, chopped

1 rounded tablespoon tamarind purée

2 dessertspoons lime juice

1 dessertspoon light soy sauce

1 dessertspoon brown sugar

1 tablespoon finely chopped fresh basil

black pepper

1 tablespoon groundnut oil

fresh basil leaves

Blend the shallots, chilli, garlic, tamarind purée, lime juice, soy sauce, sugar and chopped basil until smooth. Put in a lidded bowl with the tomato. Season with black pepper and add the courgettes. Mix well, then cover and chill for a couple of hours. Heat the oil in a wok, then stir-fry the marinated courgettes for a few minutes until tender. Garnish with fresh basil leaves when serving.

Broad beans with peas (serves 4/6)

12oz/350g shelled baby broad beans

8oz/225g shelled peas

4 shallots, peeled and chopped

2 garlic cloves, crushed

1 tablespoon groundnut oil

1 rounded tablespoon green curry paste (see page 68)

1 tablespoon light soy sauce

black pepper

green chilli rings

finely chopped fresh coriander

Steam the broad beans, rinse under cold running water and carefully remove the skins. Cook the peas. Stir-fry the shallots and garlic in the oil until tender, then add the curry paste and stir around for 1 minute. Mix in the broad beans, peas and soy sauce, season with black pepper and stir around for a minute or so. Transfer to a serving dish and garnish with chilli rings and chopped coriander.

Hot gingered carrots (serves 4/6)

1lb/450g carrots, scraped, halved lengthways and sliced

1½ inch/3cm piece of root ginger, grated

2 shallots, peeled and finely chopped

1 garlic clove, crushed

1 dessertspoon groundnut oil

2 dried bird's-eye chillies, crushed

6 tablespoons water

1 tablespoon light soy sauce

black pepper

finely chopped fresh coriander

Fry the ginger, shallots and garlic in the oil until softened. Add the carrots, chillies, water and soy sauce and season with black pepper. Stir well, raise the heat and cook until just tender. Spoon into a dish and garnish with fresh coriander.

Sweet and sour vegetables (serves 4/6)

1¼ lb/550g mixed prepared vegetables (e.g. celery, courgette, peppers, mushrooms, baby sweetcorn), cut into even-sized pieces

2 shallots, peeled and finely chopped

1 lemon grass stalk, finely chopped

1 small red chilli, finely chopped

1 inch/2.5cm piece of root ginger, finely chopped

2 garlic cloves, crushed

1 tablespoon groundnut oil

4 fl.oz/125ml water

1 rounded dessertspoon tamarind purée

1 tablespoon rice vinegar

1 tablespoon lime juice

1 dessertspoon light soy sauce

1 rounded teaspoon cornflour

1 teaspoon brown sugar

finely sliced spring onions

Heat the oil and fry the shallots, lemon grass, chilli, ginger and garlic for 2 minutes. Dissolve the tamarind purée in the water and add to the pan together with the chopped vegetables. Stir well and bring to the boil. Cover and simmer, stirring occasionally, until almost tender. Mix the vinegar with the lime juice, soy sauce, cornflour and brown sugar until smooth, stir into the vegetables and continue simmering for a minute or so until the mixture thickens. Transfer to a serving bowl and garnish with sliced spring onions.

Green beans with coconut and peanut dressing (serves 4/6)

1lb/450g green beans, topped, tailed and cut into 2 inch/5cm
   lengths

½oz/15g creamed coconut, grated

½oz/15g roasted peanuts, finely chopped

¼ teaspoon crushed dried chillies

2 dessertspoons lime juice

2 dessertspoons light soy sauce

2 dessertspoons water

1 dessertspoon brown sugar

finely chopped fresh coriander

Mix the creamed coconut with the peanuts, chilli, lime juice, soy sauce, water and sugar until well combined. Steam the grean beans until just done, then add the dressing and toss thoroughly. Garnish with chopped coriander.

Steamed kale with coriander and garlic (serves 4/6)

1lb/450g kale

2 rounded dessertspoons coriander and garlic dressing (see page 103)

2 dessertspoons rice vinegar

1 dessertspoon groundnut oil

2 shallots, peeled and finely chopped

crispy fried garlic (see page 102)

Remove the thick stalks from the kale, shred the leaves and steam them. Meanwhile fry the shallots in the oil until soft and mix the coriander and garlic dressing with the vinegar. Add the steamed kale and dressing to the shallots and toss well before transferring to a serving dish. Use crispy fried garlic as garnish.

Mangetout, mushroom and water chestnut stir-fry (serves 4/6)

8oz/225g mangetout, topped, tailed and cut into 1 inch/2.5cm diagonal slices

4oz/100g mushrooms, wiped and sliced

8oz/225g tin water chestnuts, drained, rinsed and sliced

1 shallot, peeled and finely chopped

2 garlic cloves, crushed

1 dessertspoon groundnut oil

1 dessertspoon sesame oil

1 tablespoon light soy sauce

roasted sesame seeds

Heat the groundnut oil in a wok and stir-fry the shallot and garlic for 2 minutes. Add the sesame oil and mangetout and fry gently until almost tender, then put in the mushrooms and water chestnuts and continue stir-frying until done. Stir in the soy sauce, spoon into a serving dish and garnish with roasted sesame seeds.

Stir-fried aubergine with tomato and chilli sauce (serves 4/6)

1½lb/675g aubergine, diced

4 tablespoons groundnut oil

6 shallots, peeled and finely chopped

6 kaffir lime leaves

1 quantity of tomato and chilli sauce (see page 105)

red chilli rings

shredded fresh basil leaves

Stir-fry the aubergine and shallots in the oil for 10 minutes. Add the lime leaves and tomato and chilli sauce and continue cooking, stirring occasionally, until just tender. Transfer to a serving dish and garnish with red chilli rings and shredded basil leaves.

Steamed vegetables with satay sauce (serves 4/6)

1½lb/675g prepared vegetables (e.g. carrot, cauliflower, courgette, mangetout, baby sweetcorn, peppers, broccoli), cut into even-sized pieces

1 quantity of satay sauce (see page 104)

crispy fried shallots and garlic (see page 102)

Steam the vegetables until just cooked. Meanwhile, heat the sauce in a large pan, then remove from the heat and add the vegetables. Mix well and put in a dish. Garnish with crispy fried shallots and garlic.

SALADS

Not only salads made with vegetables, but salads made from fresh tropical fruits also are typical of the many varieties enjoyed in Thailand. Some are made with one fruit only, others are savoury mixed fruit salads, which can be easily prepared from a selection of fruits of your choice, such as mango, papaya, pineapple, banana, lychees, melon and starfruit, and dressed with one of the savoury dressings or dipping sauces from pages 103–107. Salads are served as accompaniments to snacks and also always included as part of the main meal. Thai cooks try to achieve a contrasting balance of colours and flavours that will complement the other dishes.

Aubergine and tofu salad (serves 4)

8oz/225g aubergine, diced

4oz/100g tomato, skinned and finely chopped

2oz/50g marinated tofu, diced

2 shallots, peeled and finely chopped

1 garlic clove, crushed

½ small red chilli, finely chopped

2 tablespoons finely chopped fresh coriander

1 tablespoon ground roasted rice (see page 102)

1 dessertspoon tamarind purée

1 dessertspoon rice vinegar

1 dessertspoon sesame oil

fresh coriander leaves

Steam the aubergine until just tender. Put in a bowl, cover and refrigerate until cold. Mix the oil with the vinegar and tamarind purée and combine with the tomato, shallots, garlic, chilli and chopped coriander. Add the aubergine, tofu and ground rice and mix thoroughly. Spoon into a serving bowl and garnish with coriander leaves.

Pomelo salad (serves 4)

1 pomelo

4 shallots, peeled

2 garlic cloves, crushed

1oz/25g roasted peanuts, chopped

2 rounded tablespoons finely chopped fresh coriander

2 dessertspoons groundnut oil

2 dessertspoons brown sugar

2 dessertspoons lime juice

2 dried bird's-eye chillies, crushed

black pepper

red chilli rings

fresh coriander leaves

finely grated lime peel

Peel the pomelo and remove all the pith and membranes. Chop the segments and put them in a mixing bowl. Cut a few thin rings from one of the shallots and set aside for garnish. Finely chop the rest of the shallots and add to the bowl together with the garlic, peanuts and chopped coriander. Mix the oil with the sugar, lime juice and dried chillies, season with black pepper and spoon over the salad. Toss well. Garnish with the shallot rings and with chilli rings, lime peel and coriander leaves.

Cucumber and radish salad (serves 4)

6oz/175g cucumber, finely chopped

6oz/175g radishes, finely chopped

4 spring onions, trimmed and finely chopped

1 green chilli, finely chopped

1 inch/2.5cm piece of root ginger, grated

1 garlic clove, crushed

2 tablespoons finely chopped fresh coriander

2 dessertspoons rice vinegar

1 dessertspoon sesame oil

black pepper

quartered cherry tomatoes

Mix the cucumber, radishes, spring onions and coriander in a large bowl. Combine the chilli with the ginger, garlic, vinegar and oil and season with black pepper. Add to the salad and toss thoroughly. Transfer to a serving bowl and garnish with quartered cherry tomatoes.

Green mango salad (serves 4)

1 medium green mango, peeled, stoned and finely chopped

2 shallots, peeled and finely chopped

1 red chilli, finely chopped

1oz/25g roasted peanuts, chopped

2 tablespoons ground roasted rice (see page 102)

2 tablespoons lime juice

2 tablespoons brown sugar

shredded Chinese leaves

fresh mint leaves

Put the mango, shallots, chilli, peanuts, ground rice, lime juice and sugar in a mixing bowl and combine well. Arrange the Chinese leaves on a serving plate and pile the salad on top. Garnish with fresh mint leaves.

Broccoli, red pepper and sesame salad (serves 4)

12oz/350g broccoli, chopped

8oz/225g red pepper

4 spring onions, trimmed and finely sliced

¼oz/7g roasted sesame seeds

2 dried bird's-eye chillies, crushed

1 tablespoon sesame oil

1 tablespoon rice vinegar

1 tablespoon light soy sauce

1 garlic clove, crushed

6 slices of cucumber, halved

Steam the broccoli for about 3 minutes until softened, then rinse under cold running water to refresh. Drain well and put in a large bowl with the spring onions. Cut four thin rings from the pepper for garnish, chop the remainder and add to the bowl. Mix the sesame oil, chillies, vinegar, soy sauce and garlic, then spoon over the salad. Add the sesame seeds and toss well. Transfer to a serving bowl, arrange the cucumber slices around the edge and garnish with the pepper rings.

Green vegetable salad (serves 4/6)

8oz/225g shelled broad beans
8oz/225g broccoli, chopped
4oz/100g green pepper, chopped
2oz/50g cucumber, chopped
2 shallots, peeled and finely chopped
1 green chilli, finely chopped
2 garlic cloves, crushed
2 rounded tablespoons finely chopped fresh coriander
1 tablespoon sesame oil
1 dessertspoon lime juice
1 dessertspoon light soy sauce
1 dessertspoon rice vinegar
1 dessertspoon brown sugar
black pepper
chopped roasted peanuts

Steam the broad beans, rinse in cold water and carefully remove the skins. Put the beans in a mixing bowl with the green pepper, cucumber, shallots, chilli, garlic and coriander. Lightly steam the broccoli to soften slightly, then rinse under cold running water and add. Combine the sesame oil with the lime juice, soy sauce, vinegar and sugar and pour over the salad. Season with black pepper and mix thoroughly. Serve in a bowl, garnished with chopped peanuts.

Papaya salad (serves 4)

1 unripe papaya, peeled, deseeded and grated

2 shallots, peeled and grated

1 red chilli, finely chopped

1 garlic clove, crushed

½ inch/1cm piece of root ginger, grated

1 tablespoon finely chopped fresh coriander

1 rounded tablespoon ground roasted rice (see page 102)

1 tablespoon lime juice

1 tablespoon brown sugar

shredded Chinese leaves

chopped roasted peanuts

Mix the papaya with the shallots, chilli, garlic, ginger, coriander, ground rice, lime juice and brown sugar. Arrange some shredded Chinese leaves on a serving plate, pile the salad on top and sprinkle with chopped peanuts.

Beansprout, mango and peanut salad (serves 4/6)

12oz/350g beansprouts

8oz/225g mango flesh, finely chopped

3oz/75g roasted peanuts, chopped

3oz/75g cucumber, finely chopped

1 red chilli, finely chopped

2 garlic cloves, crushed

3 tablespoons finely chopped fresh coriander

1 tablespoon sesame oil

1 tablespoon light soy sauce

1 tablespoon rice vinegar

finely sliced spring onions

Blanch the beansprouts in boiling water for 1 minute, drain and rinse under cold running water. Drain well and put in a mixing bowl with the mango, cucumber, chilli and coriander. Combine the sesame oil with the soy sauce, rice vinegar and garlic and add to the salad, together with the peanuts. Toss thoroughly, spoon into a serving bowl and garnish with sliced spring onions.

Vegetable rice salad (serves 4)

4oz/100g Thai jasmine rice

4oz/100g shelled broad beans

4oz/100g red pepper, finely chopped

4oz/100g sweetcorn kernels

2 spring onions, trimmed and finely sliced

1 green chilli, finely chopped

1 inch/2.5cm piece of root ginger, grated

1 garlic clove, crushed

2 tablespoons finely chopped fresh coriander

1 dessertspoon sesame oil

1 dessertspoon rice vinegar

1 dessertspoon light soy sauce

1 tomato, cut into thin wedges

roasted cashew nuts

Cook the rice, drain and rinse under cold running water, drain well and put in a large bowl. Cook the broad beans until tender, then rinse in cold water and carefully remove the skins. Add the beans, red pepper, spring onions, chilli and coriander to the rice. Cook the sweetcorn kernels, rinse under cold water and add. Combine the garlic, ginger, oil, rice vinegar and soy sauce, pour over the salad and mix well. Put into a serving bowl, arrange the tomato wedges around the edge and sprinkle cashew nuts on top.

Pineapple and water chestnut salad (serves 4)

4oz/100g pineapple flesh, finely chopped

4oz/100g tinned water chestnuts, drained and sliced

4oz/100g cucumber, finely chopped

1oz/25g cellophane noodles

1oz/25g roasted cashews, chopped

2 spring onions, trimmed and finely sliced

1 tablespoon ground roasted rice (see page 102)

1 inch/2.5cm piece of root ginger, grated

1 dried bird's-eye chilli, crushed

1 tablespoon lime juice

1 tablespoon rice vinegar

1 dessertspoon soy sauce

1 dessertspoon lemon grass purée

1 teaspoon brown sugar

finely chopped fresh coriander

Soak the noodles in boiling water for 5 minutes, drain and rinse. Drain again and chop into short lengths, then put them in a bowl with the pineapple, water chestnuts, cucumber and spring onions. Mix the root ginger, chilli, lime juice, vinegar, soy sauce, lemon grass purée and sugar and add to the salad together with the cashews and ground rice. Toss well and serve garnished with chopped coriander.

Mangetout, bamboo shoot and baby corn salad (serves 4/6)

4oz/100g mangetout, topped, tailed and cut into 1 inch/2.5cm diagonal slices

8oz/225g tin sliced bamboo shoots, drained, rinsed and cut into 1 inch/2.5cm diagonal slices

4oz/100g baby sweetcorn, sliced

4oz/100g tomato, skinned and finely chopped

4 spring onions, trimmed and finely sliced

1 garlic clove, crushed

1 inch/2.5cm piece of root ginger, grated

1 red chilli

1 dessertspoon sesame oil

1 dessertspoon lime juice

1 dessertspoon rice vinegar

1 dessertspoon light soy sauce

1 teaspoon brown sugar

shredded fresh basil leaves

Steam the mangetout and baby corn to soften slightly, then rinse under cold running water to refresh. Drain and put in a mixing bowl with the bamboo shoots, spring onions and garlic. Cut a few rings from the chilli for garnish, finely chop the rest and add to the bowl. Mix the tomato with the ginger, sesame oil, lime juice, vinegar, soy sauce and sugar, add to the salad and toss thoroughly. Spoon into a serving bowl and garnish with the chilli rings and with shredded basil leaves.

Mushroom, coriander and garlic salad
(serves 4)

12oz/350g mushrooms, wiped and sliced

2 shallots, peeled and finely chopped

1 lemon grass stalk, finely chopped

1 dried bird's-eye chilli, crushed

1 tablespoon ground roasted rice (see page 102)

1 dessertspoon groundnut oil

2 tablespoons coriander and garlic dressing (see page 103)

1 tablespoon rice vinegar

fresh coriander leaves

crispy fried garlic (see page 102)

Heat the oil and fry the shallots and lemon grass stalk until soft, then add the mushrooms and fry until the juices begin to run. Remove from the heat and stir in the crushed chilli and ground rice. Mix the coriander and garlic dressing with the vinegar and add. Toss well, transfer to a serving bowl, cover and allow to cool. Garnish with fresh coriander and crispy fried garlic before serving.

ACCOMPANIMENTS

No Thai meal is considered complete without a selection of dressings and dipping sauces, made from basic flavourings and served in little bowls for diners to spoon over or dip foods into. Really basic condiments can include chopped chillies, garlic or ginger steeped in soy sauce or rice vinegar or in a mixture of these. Bowls of roasted nuts and seeds are often served, to sprinkle over dishes at the table. Although Thai cuisine is not noted for a wide range of speciality breads, one that is particularly popular is a pan-fried flat bread used to scoop up rice and curries.

Pan-fried bread (makes 8)

8oz/225g plain flour
pinch of salt
approx. 4 fl.oz/125ml water
groundnut oil

Mix the flour with the salt and add enough water to bind into a dough. Turn this out onto a floured board and knead well, then return it to the bowl, cover and leave for 30 minutes. Divide the dough into 8 equal pieces and roll each one first into a ball and then into a circle of about 6 inches/15cm. Leave the rounds for 10 minutes, then brush them with groundnut oil on both sides. Brush a wok with groundnut oil and heat until hot. Fry the breads for a few minutes on each side, pressing down on them with a spatula, until golden speckled. Serve warm.

Ground roasted rice

raw glutinous rice

Dry-fry the rice grains, stirring constantly, in a heavy-based pan until golden. Grind the rice to a powder either with a pestle in a mortar or in a nut mill. Store in an airtight container in the fridge for up to 2 weeks.

Crispy fried garlic, onion and shallots

finely sliced garlic cloves
finely sliced onions and shallots
groundnut oil

Heat some oil in a wok and fry the garlic and onions and shallots separately until golden brown and crispy. Beware, garlic browns much quicker than onions and shallots. Drain and pat dry on kitchen paper. Serve cold as a garnish.

Roasted nuts and seeds

raw peanuts, cashew nuts or sesame seeds

Dry-fry the nuts or seeds in a wok or frying pan, stirring them around constantly until evenly golden. Allow to cool before serving. Can be stored in an airtight container in the fridge for up to 2 weeks. For crushed nuts, put them into a food bag and crush into tiny pieces with a rolling pin.

Coriander and garlic dressing (serves 4)

2oz/50g fresh coriander stalks and leaves, chopped

8 garlic cloves, crushed

1 dessertspoon black peppercorns

Blend the ingredients until a paste forms. Spoon into soups, cooked rice or noodles, or simply serve as a condiment.

Red chilli and tamarind dressing (serves 4)

2 red chillies, finely chopped

2 rounded tablespoons tamarind purée

2 tablespoons dark soy sauce

1 tablespoon rice wine

1 tablespoon rice vinegar

Mix the ingredients well and transfer to a small bowl.

Sesame and garlic dressing (serves 4)

½oz/15g roasted sesame seeds

2 dessertspoons sesame oil

2 dessertspoons rice wine

1 dessertspoon light soy sauce

1 tablespoon rice vinegar

2 garlic cloves, crushed

Mix all the ingredients until well combined.

Green mango and lime sauce (serves 4)

1 small green mango, peeled, stoned and grated

2 garlic cloves, crushed

2 tablespoons lime juice

1 rounded tablespoon brown sugar

1 teaspoon light soy sauce

¼ teaspoon crushed dried red chilli

Combine the ingredients thoroughly and put in a serving bowl.

Satay sauce (serves 4)

2oz/50g roasted peanuts, ground

6 fl.oz/175ml coconut milk

1 rounded dessertspoon red curry paste (see page 68)

1 dessertspoon tamarind purée

1 dessertspoon lime juice

1 dessertspoon groundnut oil

2 shallots, peeled and finely chopped

1 garlic clove, crushed

black pepper

Heat the oil in a pan and fry the shallots and garlic until soft, then remove from the heat and add the remaining ingredients. Mix thoroughly and return to the heat. Bring to the boil while stirring and continue stirring for a few seconds until the sauce thickens. Serve warm.

Tomato and chilli sauce (serves 4)

12oz/350g ripe tomatoes, skinned and finely chopped

1 red chilli, finely chopped

2 spring onions, trimmed and finely chopped

2 garlic cloves, crushed

3 tablespoons finely chopped fresh coriander

1 tablespoon tamarind purée

1 tablespoon rice vinegar

black pepper

Mix all of the ingredients until well combined. Transfer to a bowl, cover and chill before serving.

Ginger dipping sauce (serves 4)

4 shallots, peeled and chopped

2 inch/5cm piece of root ginger, finely chopped

1 teaspoon crushed dried chillies

2 tablespoons lime juice

2 tablespoons brown sugar

4 tablespoons water

2 dessertspoons light soy sauce

black pepper

Put the ingredients in a blender and blend smooth.

Sweet chilli and garlic dipping sauce (serves 4)

2oz/50g red chillies, finely chopped

4 garlic cloves, crushed

1 tablespoon brown sugar

1 tablespoon sesame oil

1 tablespoon light soy sauce

2 tablespoons rice vinegar

4 fl.oz/125ml water

Bring all the ingredients to the boil in a small pan. Cover and simmer for 10 minutes, then pour into a bowl and allow to cool before serving.

Tamarind and shallot dipping sauce (serves 4)

3 shallots, peeled and finely chopped

1 red chilli, deseeded and finely chopped

2 garlic cloves, crushed

2 tablespoons tamarind purée

4 tablespoons water

1 tablespoon rice vinegar

1 dessertspoon brown sugar

1 dessertspoon groundnut oil

Fry the shallots, chilli and garlic in the oil until soft. Remove from the heat, add the remaining ingredients and mix thoroughly. Put into a serving bowl, cover and allow to cool.

Coconut and lime dipping sauce (serves 4)

½oz/15g creamed coconut, grated

1 garlic clove, crushed

1 dried bird's-eye chilli, crushed

2 tablespoons lime juice

1 dessertspoon brown sugar

5 fl.oz/150ml hot water

1 round teaspoon cornflour

black pepper

Mix the ingredients in a small pan until smooth. Bring to the boil while stirring, then transfer to a bowl, cover and leave to cool before serving.

DESSERTS

Sweet dessert-type dishes are very popular in Thailand, especially those flavoured with coconut, a favourite ingredient in both sweet and savoury dishes. As is the case in many other Asian countries, these dishes are more likely to be served as snacks throughout the day than after meals. If dessert is offered it is usually a simple selection of fresh fruits, rather than a more elaborate dish.

Fresh fruit platter with lychee and lime sorbet (serves 4)

a selection of fresh fruits such as mango, pineapple, papaya,
    melon, star fruit, banana

lime juice

finely grated lime peel

sorbet

14oz/400g tin of lychees in syrup

2 dessertspoons lime juice

Blend the lychees and syrup smooth with the lime juice. Pour into four 3 inch/8cm diameter ramekin dishes, cover and freeze for a few hours until just firm.

Peel and deseed the fruits where necessary and cut into even-sized slices or chunks. Arrange a selection of fruit on 4 serving plates and sprinkle with lime juice. Run a sharp knife around the edges of the sorbets to loosen, then turn them out onto the plates. If the sorbets have become too hard, keep them at room temperature for 30 minutes before serving. Garnish with the grated lime peel.

Pumpkin and coconut pudding (serves 4)

1lb/450g firm pumpkin flesh, diced

10 fl.oz/300ml coconut milk

½oz/15g brown sugar

toasted flaked coconut

Mix the sugar with the coconut milk, add the pumpkin and bring to the boil. Simmer uncovered for 8-10 minutes, stirring occasionally, until the pumpkin is tender. Take out the pumpkin with a slotted spoon and divide it between 4 glass dishes. Boil the remaining liquid while stirring until it thickens. Spoon over the pumpkin, then cover and refrigerate until cold. Garnish with toasted flaked coconut before serving.

Bananas in coconut milk with ginger (serves 4)

1½lb/675g bananas, peeled and thickly sliced

6 fl.oz/175ml coconut milk

sliced stem ginger

toasted flaked coconut

Put the bananas and coconut milk in a pan and bring to the boil. Lower the heat and simmer, stirring constantly, for 2-3 minutes until the bananas have softened. Divide between 4 bowls and garnish with stem ginger and flaked coconut. Serve warm.

Coconut custards (serves 4)

16 fl.oz/475ml soya milk

1oz/25g creamed coconut

1oz/25g cornflour

½oz/15g brown sugar

1 teaspoon vanilla extract

toasted desiccated coconut

Put the creamed coconut in a double boiler and heat gently until melted. Mix the cornflour with the soya milk until smooth and add to the pan, together with the sugar and vanilla extract. Mix until well combined, raise the heat and bring to the boil while stirring constantly. Continue stirring until the custard thickens, then pour into four 3 inch/8cm diameter ramekin dishes. Cover and put in the fridge for a few hours or overnight until cold and set. Serve garnished with toasted coconut.

Sticky rice with mango (serves 4)

4oz/100g glutinous rice

4 fl.oz/125ml coconut milk

1oz/25g brown sugar

1 ripe mango, peeled, stoned and sliced

Rinse the rice, put it in a pan of water, cover and leave to soak overnight. Drain and rinse the rice again, then steam until done. Mix the coconut milk with the sugar and bring to the boil. Remove from the heat and stir in the steamed rice. Cover and allow to cool for about 1 hour, by which time the coconut milk will have been absorbed.

Divide the rice between 4 serving bowls and top each one with chilled slices of mango.

Melon and ginger sorbet (serves 4/6)

1lb/450g melon flesh, chopped

1oz/25g brown sugar

2 inch/5cm piece of root ginger, finely grated

2 fl.oz/50ml water

sliced stem ginger

Bring the sugar, grated root ginger and water to the boil in a small pan. Transfer to a blender, add the chopped melon and blend smooth. Pour into a shallow freezerproof container. Cover and freeze for 2 hours, then whisk well and return to the freezer for a few hours until just frozen. Leave the sorbet at room temperature for 30 minutes before serving if it has become too solid. Scoop the sorbet into bowls and garnish with sliced stem ginger.

Baked black rice pudding (serves 4)

4oz/100g black glutinous rice

12 fl.oz/350ml thin coconut milk

5 fl.oz/150ml soya milk

1oz/25g brown sugar

¼ teaspoon ground cinnamon

Put all the ingredients in a saucepan and stir well. Bring to the boil, then transfer to a greased 6 inch/15cm round baking dish. Bake in a preheated oven at 150°C/300°F/Gas mark 2 for 20 minutes. Remove from the oven and stir well, then return to the oven for another 20-25 minutes until set. Serve warm, garnished with fresh fruits.

Battered bananas (serves 4)

1lb/450g bananas, peeled and cut into chunks

4oz/100g ground roasted rice (see page 102)

1oz/25g creamed coconut, grated

4 fl.oz/125ml soya milk

¼ teaspoon ground cinnamon

groundnut oil

extra ground cinnamon

Mix the ground rice, coconut and ¼ teaspoonful of ground cinnamon with the soya milk until smooth. Add the banana chunks and combine until they are coated with the batter. Heat a small amount of oil in a wok. Spoon the coated banana chunks into the pan and fry for a few minutes until golden. Turn the pieces and fry until browned all over. Serve hot, sprinkled with ground cinnamon.

Pineapple rice pudding (serves 4)

3oz/75g short grain rice

1oz/25g brown sugar

6 fl.oz/175ml pineapple juice

10 fl.oz/300ml soya milk

4oz/100g pineapple flesh, finely chopped

Wash the rice and put it in a pan with the pineapple juice. Bring to the boil and simmer for 10 minutes, then remove from the heat and stir in the sugar and soya milk. Return to the cooker and simmer very gently, stirring occasionally, for about 25 minutes until the liquid has been absorbed and the rice is done. Spoon into 4 bowls and garnish with the chopped pineapple.

Mango and coconut ice (serves 6)

12oz/350g ripe mango flesh, chopped

14 fl.oz/400ml coconut milk

1 rounded tablespoon demerara sugar

fresh mango slices

toasted flaked coconut

Blend the chopped mango with the coconut milk and sugar until smooth. Pour into a shallow freezerproof container, cover and freeze for 5-6 hours until just frozen. If it become too hard keep at room temperature for an hour before serving. Serve scoops of the ice, topped with fresh mango slices and toasted flaked coconut.

Baked mung custards (serves 4)

2oz/50g mung beans

1oz/25g ground roasted rice (see page 102)

½oz/15g creamed coconut, grated

½oz/15g brown sugar

8 fl.oz/225ml soya milk

¼ teaspoon ground cinnamon

toasted desiccated coconut

Cook the mung beans, drain in a sieve and press out any excess water. Mash the beans and blend them smooth with the ground rice, creamed coconut, sugar, soya milk and cinnamon. Pour the mixture into four 2½ inch/6cm diameter ramekin dishes and place them on a baking sheet. Bake in a preheated oven at 180°C/350°F/Gas mark 4 for 20 minutes until set. Allow to cool for 30 minutes, then garnish with toasted coconut and serve with fresh fruit.

Banana and coconut pancakes (serves 4)

12oz/350g ripe bananas, peeled and mashed

4oz/100g plain flour

10 fl.oz/300ml soya milk

1oz/25g creamed coconut, grated

groundnut oil

lime juice

brown sugar

Mix the flour with the soya milk and coconut until smooth, then add the banana and combine thoroughly. Heat a small amount of oil in a wok and drop tablespoonfuls of the mixture into the oil, allowing room for spreading. Fry for a few minutes until golden brown, then carefully turn each pancake over and fry the other side. Serve the pancakes hot, sprinkled with lime juice and brown sugar.

FRUIT COCKTAILS

Freshly made fruit cocktails are legendary in Thailand and they are blended from all sorts of fruits that grow abundantly in the tropical conditions. Full of flavour and refreshingly thirst-quenching, fruit cocktails can be bought ready-made from the humblest roadside stall or are made at home and served with meals and snacks.

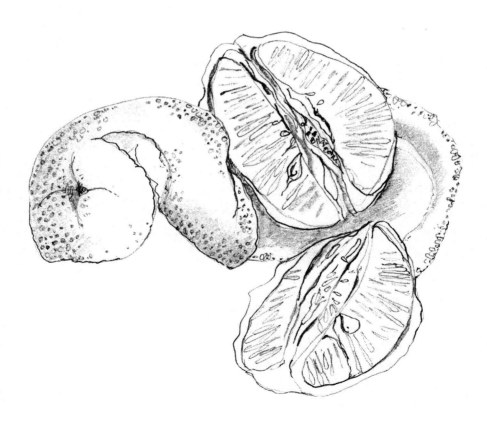

Mango, orange and lime (serves 4)

4oz/100g ripe mango flesh, chopped

10 fl.oz/300ml chilled sparkling mineral water

12 fl.oz/350ml fresh orange juice

1 rounded tablespoon brown sugar

2 tablespoons lime juice

crushed ice

Blend the mango, orange juice, sugar and lime juice smooth. Pour into a large jug, cover and refrigerate until cold. Add the mineral water and whisk until well combined, then pour into glasses and add crushed ice.

Melon and ginger (serves 4)

4oz/100g melon flesh, chopped

2 inch/5cm piece of root ginger, finely chopped

24 fl.oz/725ml water

1 rounded tablespoon brown sugar

melon balls

crushed ice

Bring the water, ginger and sugar to the boil and simmer for 3 minutes. Remove from the heat and allow to cool, then strain the liquid into a blender and add the chopped melon. Blend until smooth and chill. Stir well, pour into glasses and add melon balls and crushed ice.

Pineapple and coconut (serves 4)

8oz/225g tin chopped pineapple in natural juice

10 fl.oz/300ml thin coconut milk

8 fl.oz/225ml chilled sparkling mineral water

crushed ice

Put the pineapple and juice and the coconut milk in a blender and blend until smooth. Chill for a couple of hours, then add the mineral water and mix until well combined. Add crushed ice when serving.

Lychee and lime (serves 4)

8 fresh lychees, peeled and stoned

1 lime, peeled

20 fl.oz/600ml water

1oz/25g brown sugar

crushed ice

4 lime slices

Chop the lime into segments and put them in a saucepan with the water and sugar. Bring to the boil, cover and simmer gently for 5 minutes. Allow to cool, then keep in the fridge until cold. Strain the juice into a blender, pressing out as much liquid as possible with the back of a spoon. Chop the lychees and add. Blend until smooth, strain the liquid into a jug and stir well. Add crushed ice and garnish each glass with a slice of lime.

Coconut and banana (serves 4)

20 fl.oz/600ml thin coconut milk, chilled

10oz/300g ripe banana, peeled and chopped

8 fl.oz/225ml chilled mineral water

ground cinnamon

Blend the banana with the coconut milk and water. Pour into glasses and sprinkle lightly with ground cinnamon.

Papaya and apple (serves 4)

8oz/225g ripe papaya flesh, chopped

16 fl.oz/475ml fresh apple juice

8 fl.oz/225ml chilled mineral water

crushed ice

Blend the papaya, apple juice and water smooth. Put some crushed ice in each glass when serving.

Lemon and orange (serves 4)

2 lemons, peeled

20 fl.oz/600ml water

1oz/25g brown sugar

8 fl.oz/225ml chilled fresh orange juice

crushed ice

lemon or orange slices

Chop the lemon segments and put them in a pan with the water and sugar. Bring to the boil, cover and simmer for 5 minutes, then allow to cool and refrigerate until cold. Strain through a fine sieve, pressing out as much liquid as possible with the back of a spoon. Add the orange juice and mix well. Pour into glasses, add crushed ice and garnish each glass with a slice of lemon or orange.

Watermelon and tamarind (serves 4)

1lb/450g watermelon flesh

2 rounded dessertspoons brown sugar

1 tablespoon tamarind purée

8 ice cubes

10 fl.oz/300ml chilled mineral water

Remove any pips from the watermelon, chop the flesh and put it in a blender with the remaining ingredients. Blend until smooth.